Never Give In

THE 12 COMMANDO RULES FOR LIFE

Major Scotty Mills

**SIMON &
SCHUSTER**

London · New York · Sydney · Toronto · New Delhi

First published in Great Britain by Simon & Schuster UK Ltd, 2022

Copyright © Scott Mills, 2022

The right of Scott Mills to be identified
as the author of this work has been asserted in accordance
with the Copyright, Designs and Patents Act, 1988.

1 3 5 7 9 10 8 6 4 2

Simon & Schuster UK Ltd
1st Floor
222 Gray's Inn Road
London WC1X 8HB

www.simonandschuster.co.uk
www.simonandschuster.com.au
www.simonandschuster.co.in

Simon & Schuster Australia, Sydney
Simon & Schuster India, New Delhi

The author and publishers have made all reasonable efforts
to contact copyright-holders for permission, and apologise
for any omissions or errors in the form of credits given.
Corrections may be made to future printings.

A CIP catalogue record for this book
is available from the British Library

Hardback ISBN: 978-1-3985-0844-6
eBook ISBN: 978-1-3985-0845-3

Typeset in Bembo by M Rules
Printed and bound in the UK using 100% Renewable
Electricity at CPI Group (UK) Ltd

MIX
Paper | Supporting
responsible forestry
FSC
www.fsc.org
FSC® C171272

For my darling Suzanne and our family – my love for you knows no bounds and I am so proud of you all. You are the inspiration behind all that I do.

CONTENTS

It's a State of Mind

Wearing burgundy leg warmers, two-tone bleached jeans, a Sergio Tacchini tracksuit (with detachable arms) and a loosely permed Afro sheened to perfection with soul glow: I was looking good. So I thought, anyway. At that time, I was into skating and I was carrying my brown suede Bauer skates that my nan and grandad had saved hard for me to have for Christmas. It was 1985 and, somehow, I had modelled myself on Leroy out of the hit TV series *Fame*, which featured a group of theatre and dance stars in the United States. He was a cool dude and I reckoned I was as well – but there was a world of difference between us: he had a brilliant future all mapped out, whereas I really didn't know what mine was.

But that day in 1985 would see a chance encounter that would go on to give my life direction, and a future that my teenage self could never have envisaged. As I was walking down Streatham High Street, it started to rain and – not wanting my skates to rust – I dived into the nearest shop, which just happened to be the Royal Marines recruiting office. Inside was a tall Marine sergeant with a huge handle-bar moustache. He, in turn, found himself face to face with someone who did not look like a future Marine. But the Marines look beyond the surface.

This Marine sergeant said to me, 'You look like a fit lad – can you do pull-ups?' I told him I could and then demonstrated by pumping out a few reps on the pull-up bar with my skates still draped over my shoulder. 'I see some potential in you, young man!' he declared, before asking the question that changed my life: 'Have you ever thought of joining the Marines?'

You see, it was never my intention to join the Royal Marines. In fact, as a teenager I had hardly heard of them at all, beyond the fact that they had played a big role in win-ning the Falklands War against Argentina. However, when the rain eased and I left the recruiting office, I had a deci-sion to make. Either I could continue with my life as it was, taking my chances in south London, or I could grasp with both hands this unlikely opportunity to change my life. So that's what I did. Everyone around me thought I was nuts – family, friends, my girlfriend at the time – and none of them, apart from my grandad Harry, thought that I had a chance of becoming one of Britain's elite Commando Green Berets.

Harry was my guide as a young lad, but despite all his good advice, from the age of fifteen I had been getting into some trouble. I left school at sixteen and went to Orpington College, where I met my very good mate Mark Prior. Mark's mum and dad, Mel and Colin, were lovely people and like second parents to me. Mark and I got into quite a few scrapes, including the occasional brush with the law, but Mel and Colin always bailed us out, and I've not forgotten that they were always there for me. Colin even offered me a job in his company, but after deep thought and a chat with my grandad, I decided to go for the green beret instead. My life has changed a lot since then, but I have always remembered the sage advice of Harry and Colin.

Once I had made that life-changing decision, I went back to the Streatham recruiting office with my paperwork for the interview and medical check, as well as fitness and psychometric tests. A few months later, I found myself entering the gates of the Commando Training Centre Royal Marines at Lympstone in Devon for a three-day pre-selection course (essentially a job interview), alongside a familiar face from my south London days, Pete Watts, and another guy named Phil Gilby, both of whom I would go on to serve with several times during my career. Phil was one of those very rare people who was always seeking to achieve the gold standard, even at a young age. The minimum standards expected in the Royal Marines might have been significantly higher than we tend to see elsewhere, but that wasn't enough for Phil; he wanted more, and constantly aimed to excel in all that he did. I had the same mentality; I still do, and it's the one I want you to have by the end of this book. Because striving for gold means you are giving your all. Reach for the stars and you might land in a tree; aim for a tree and you could end up on your backside. It requires courage to reach for the gold standard because you have to step outside of your comfort zone, but it pays off because you maximise your chance of success and development, whether that's personal, sporting, professional – whatever area of your life you commit to. Phil proved that and went on to be deservedly awarded an MBE for his endeavours in becoming the top non-commissioned officer in the Royal Marines as the Corps Regimental Sergeant Major.

The men running the Potential Royal Marines Course, as they call this pre-selection process, instantly stood out to me as role models. Wearing their green berets with pride, they used words that I had little to no understanding of at the time, like 'humility', 'integrity' and the phrase 'understated excellence', all of which we will come on to discuss. As I started off in Marines training, I saw these men and wanted to be like them. To achieve this, I realised that not only was I going to have to hold my actions and habits to a higher standard, but I would have to do so consistently: this was going to be a day-by-day, week-by-week journey, and would require every ounce of my effort and commitment. I completed the training, which at thirty-two weeks is the longest and hardest military basic training in the world. I earned my green beret. But that was just the start: life would never be the same again.

I want to share with you my journey. And it starts with belief. Belief in myself. Belief that I was in control of where life would take me. And if that was true for me, it is true for you too. The things I have gone on to achieve since earning the green beret, the places I have been, the things I have seen, the people I have met, once seemed like an impossible dream to a boy from Peckham. This was made clear to me on a school trip, when we stood outside Buckingham Palace looking through the gates admiring the Changing of the Guard and the teacher said to me: 'This as far as you will ever get. People like *you* don't ever get to go into places like *that.*' It was a judgmental statement that was designed to limit my self-belief as a child. I never forgot it. Little did that teacher know – nor my eight-year-old self, for that matter – that one day I would one day go on to dine with Her Majesty the Queen and the royal family in that very place.

In fact, one encounter with the Queen in that very palace nearly ended very badly – for both of us! I was at a special reception, taking a moment, sipping some lovely champagne as I leaned against a wall when, suddenly, I felt something move behind me. My training kicked in: I instinctively swung around with my elbow primed at head height to do damage, but thankfully it stopped just in time – about an inch from the head of the British monarch. I froze, felt a chill down my spine. The Queen, who had emerged behind me through a hidden door, gave me a nod and went about her business.

That journey, from the streets of Peckham to Buckingham Palace, was made possible through the Marines, and crucially through the core values that the Marines instilled in me. Over the years I have met many challenges, whether in my personal life or with the green beret on my head, and what I discovered is that the Commando values are not just for Marines; they're for everybody, in every circumstance.

The Royal Marines changed my life in ways I couldn't have imagined, and this book offers you the chance to transform yours through the twelve core values that I have learned along my incredible journey with them:

- RESPECT
- OVERCOMING
- SELF-DISCIPLINE
- DETERMINATION
- ADAPTABILITY
- COURAGE
- KINDNESS
- HUMILITY
- UNDERSTANDING
- CHEERFULNESS
- INTEGRITY
- EXCELLENCE

Royal Marines come from every walk of life, but what I've found is that the men with the green beret all share the same mindset, and that mindset has been shaped by these core values. Through these values comes a sense of purpose, of belonging and identity that goes beyond yourself. You too can have that mindset, to take life head on and never give in.

We're all on a journey in this life – with a past, a present and a future – and at present we are travelling through turbulent times. These values will offer a road map as we explore them across a wide range of situations and experiences. This book is here to offer a structure to not just survive but to thrive, even in the hardest of circumstances. And it is here to inspire you through the stories and lessons not just from my life, but also from the lives of many incredible people who I have been fortunate enough to encounter along the way. I realised that I cannot tell my story without telling theirs, sharing the qualities that I see in them and strive to improve upon in myself.

Toward the end of my career in the Royal Marines, I was honoured to see the fruits of this when I was awarded a national Military Award by my friend Gareth Southgate at the *Sun* newspaper's 'Millies' awards for inspiring others in their lives. During my time as a Marine and beyond, I have enjoyed being able to use these values to help develop individuals and to build winning teams, to assist young people and businesses across a multitude of different industries seeking to raise their standards, refine their values and to knit individuals together as a cohesive unit. It has all been about the pursuit of excellence in the right manner.

Because while these values are embodied by the Royal Marines, they are not exclusive to them. These qualities are universally valued and recognised, it is simply that the place I encountered them, the place where they changed my life, was in the Marines. Now I am sharing them with you in the belief that they can offer a strong foundation and opportunities for life-changing growth for anyone in the world, in any circumstance – including you.

CHAPTER 1

Respect

Definition: The deep admiration you feel
for someone as a result of their abilities,
qualities, or achievements.

The flow of respect

If you type 'respect' into the search engine of the Royal
Marines website, you will be directed to a small but powerful
section entitled 'Pride', which concludes with the profound
statement: 'This is a job where respect isn't just a possibility –
it's guaranteed.'

The honour of being part of the Marines – its history, identity and culture – consumes everyone who has ever donned
the green beret. Respect is part of the DNA of a Marine. And
today, when you cast an eye across the landscape of society

in general, it is fair to say that we are in need of a communal injection of respect – for ourselves and for each other.

In fact, I like to think of respect as *three*-way: respect for yourself, respect for others and the respect others have for you. Let's start by taking a deep look at yourself and at the people in your life. Ask yourself:

- Do you have respect for yourself?
- Do the people around you have respect for you?
- And do you respect them?

These three facets are closely linked. Where one is strengthened, the other two will also be. The common denominator between all these is this: respect is about relationships. Whether that's the relationship you have with yourself, or with those around you. And central to this, I have learnt along the way, is to treat others as you wish to be treated. This is a common phrase, but its importance cannot be overstated. Treating others as you wish to be treated means overlooking differences, valuing every individual, and showing them the respect that everyone deserves. This in turn leads to longer-lasting, more meaningful relationships that develop over time, with people from all different walks of life. Real respect is blind to colour, race, age and religion. Let's now look at where this respect stems from.

Respect in the Marines is nurtured from the ground up; it's at the grassroots, and this is a crucial element in building respect into the life of a community, whether that be the school environment, the family structure, the sports team or the corporate business. Respect is built up over time, layer upon layer, solidifying a reputation that you can be proud of, while at the same time always being aware that it can be lost in a moment. It is not something you can buy, or earn overnight, and it is not something you can expect, as if it were your right – it is something you must work at, every day, patiently and respectfully.

When I joined the Marines, I saw the commanders, I saw the respect that the new recruits had for them, and I knew that I wanted that. But this aspiration had to come from the right place. It was respect for the organisation, for my brother Marines, that was the driving force – wanting to earn respect purely for myself would not have got me anywhere. These Marines were passing the torch on to us and we would ultimately have the opportunity to do the same to new recruits further down the line, and so the bond of respect and high standards would remain unbroken. Everyone was expected to be part of adding to the 350-year legacy of this great organisation. The Marine Corps consistently drills home to you the importance of putting others ahead of yourself, being polite and considering others: in other words, practising respect. And the key word here is practising. At every stage, you have to think of the effects of your actions before you do make them. The Marines ethos encapsulates this, and demands that you show respect at every juncture. Respect is at the core of life in the Marines. Is it at the core of your life? And if not, why not?

This was a key starting point in my adult life, and I quickly learned that you show respect by what you do and how you do it – and this is also exactly how you *earn* respect.

Let's look now at how you grow this respect.

The importance of role models

When looking at personal growth, the perceived wisdom is often that it comes from within, from the self. But while self-respect is crucial, sometimes we have to look outside ourselves to first nurture that seed of respect. We look to people we feel respect for: role models. This is because as your respect for others grows, and you find yourself learning from and emulating those role models, so will your self-respect grow, and in turn the respect that others have for you.

Role models are critical. If you have no proper role model at home and you don't listen to role models in school, then how do you learn to both give and receive respect? The first step is therefore in seeking out those whom you respect – whether that is at home, among your friends or peers, in the workplace or wider afield, such as a figure in a public role.

When I think back to my days in school, I recall that I didn't particularly respect myself as a youngster starting out. I can't think of any older kid who was a role model and the attitude of some of my teachers was in fact very damaging to my sense of self-respect. One teacher outright told me I wouldn't amount to much and I was starting to believe it. This is an important lesson: don't internalise the attitude of those you don't respect. Instead, look around for those you do respect and whose opinion is therefore valuable to you. I was very fortunate to have several special people in my life, two of whom were my grandparents Harry and Edie Mills, who always encouraged me to live right and gave me a good set of values, which the Marines built upon. One thing Harry always emphasised to me was respect. He never lied. He wasn't big-headed; he had no ego, was always humble, and that stuck with me.

I never knew my father. My mother Vivien was the inspiration for my love of sport, as she was extremely talented and competed in sprinting and long jump for England, as well as being a busy legal secretary. I recall many special evenings with her watching the athletics at Crystal Palace dreaming of being the next Daley Thompson or Carl Lewis. When I was about five, my mum moved out of my nan and grandad's house and I was brought up by them. Mum eventually married and I'm fortunate to have two brothers, Tim and Alex, as well as a sister, Lola, all of whom are extremely talented and successful in their own right. I'm very proud of them all and their children and we are a close-knit family.

It was my grandad Harry, however, who was my mentor, guide and role model. Growing up as a teenager in south London, I was part of a tough group of Millwall supporters. I'm sure if you saw me back then you might have dismissed me as a hooligan. I was doing stupid things, getting into fights and generally making poor life choices. Although I was getting into some bother, I was blessed to have Harry as a father figure and best mate. He was my hero, so when I got into trouble, I never wanted him to find out as I felt I was letting him down. Having respect for him was sowing the first seeds of having respect for myself, and learning to recognise when I fell short of that.

A 5ft 2in Londoner with nineteen tattoos, Harry had a life story that commanded respect. He was born in 1912 and, as a corporal in the Bedfordshire and Hertfordshire Regiment, Harry experienced what must have been torrid times in the battle of Monte Cassino and at Dunkirk during the Second World War. Although we talked a lot, he would rarely speak to me about his time in the army, but I would sometimes stumble across his medals tucked away at the back of drawers.

After serving in the war, he became a bus conductor. On school holidays he would take me along to the bus station at Catford and leave me there all day while he did his shift, and there I would play snooker and darts. I couldn't reach the full-size table, so he'd leave me a chair and I loved it. He would come off his shift and we'd go home together and play darts or cribbage. Harry spent time with me, and that's the most valuable thing you can give people. We would speak about sports but also about life. I would listen to Harry, but he would also listen to me. That's the thing about respect: it flows from one person to another and back round again. I respected Harry for the love he showed for me and the guidance he gave, and Harry respected me for the potential he saw in me.

As my role model, Harry taught me so much. Kids who don't have role models, especially those from difficult back-grounds, often also lack respect for the potential within themselves. I have seen so much wasted talent and unfulfilled potential in this world; I could easily have been one of those who went down a different, more destructive path because of how some perceived me, the lack of respect they showed me, and the lack of self-respect that in turn engendered in me.

This is not only true of young people; it is the same in the workplace, the family home, in sports or social groups. Sometimes we have to work hard to see what it is that we respect in others, or in ourselves, but it is always worth the effort. Realising that each person can bring an attribute or skill can make a real difference and add value to the effectiveness of any team. That team could be the family unit, the school, the youth club, on the street corner or in the workplace. Wherever you find yourself, respect is non-negotiable, and yet sadly we all know of examples where it seems to have crumbled.

For if respect engenders respect, the opposite is also true. There is a growing sense of belief in some working-class communities that they are not respected and so they see no point in giving that respect back. This can be so damaging. With a lack of inspirational role models for our young people to aspire to follow, they choose the path of least resistance and some fall for the imitation versions found on the streets. They look to fast-track methods to earn their fortune in a manner that breeds contempt for others. Respect is the life source for any community, small or large, and everything else springs from it – but if that source is poisoned, then that respect is lost and society becomes toxic.

I didn't get that right away, because by the time I was leaving college in 1985 the two key qualifications I had were being the college pool champion (two years in a row) and being able to drink my body weight in beer. Little did I know at that time that, three decades later, I would become a Royal Marines officer, head of physical training and performance for all of the UK's 6,500 Royal Marines, and go on to train the England football team, Rugby World Cup winners and gold-medal Olympians, break a nineteen-year-old world record, be an Olympic Games flag-bearer, go to eighty-six countries on six continents, serve in four war zones and be married with four kids!

Nothing I have achieved, no part of this life that I have enjoyed to the maximum, could have happened without respect at its core – and I found that respect in the Royal Marines.

But before the big things come to you, it is the more obvious marks of respect in getting the small actions right that truly pave the way: get the small things right now and you will be more effective when it comes to the bigger challenges this world can throw at you. An example of these small acts of respect that I learned early in my Marine training was the simple demand of being on time. In those early days of training, everyone is taking in so much information and learning to present themselves in the required manner that it is often easy to arrive late. This is soon remedied; we have a saying that a good Marine is always five minutes early – with the only exception being in the Arctic, because then you could freeze to death!

And so, when it comes to parade time, you demonstrate respect by making sure that you don't let your colleagues down by being late. Because when someone is late, the other men pay for it, often in the form of press-ups or other high-intensity exercise. The recruit who has arrived late has to stand by the side and call out the number of press-ups required. As well as that, you are often told to parade earlier the next day as a collective punishment, thereby reducing your personal time. Believe me, the sense of shame you experience means you will never do it again. This is true in everyday life – being on time shows that you respect and value other people's time and don't want to waste it. I detest lateness even to this day, and will do everything in my power to afford someone the courtesy of being five minutes early.

What small actions can you make in your daily life that show respect to those around you?

The role of the corporal

One aspect of respect that you must realise is that it is earned. To those on the outside, it may seem that simply being a Royal Marine means that someone has automatically gained ultimate respect, but that would be missing the point of the ethos of those who wear the green beret. Respect is earned, and that's how it should be – in the Marines and in civilian life. It is because respect is earned that one of the most influential roles in the Marines is the corporal; a junior leader who others look toward for direction. While it may sometimes appear as though respect is the privilege of those in the top leadership positions, it is often in middle leadership that respect is most crucial. Let me explain.

The corporals are the first-level leaders who command respect, but as they are not at the top of the chain, this respect has to be earned; the rank itself is not enough to command respect unless it is backed up by action. As the first point of contact for those who are at the entry level of the Marines, it is the corporal's job to both demonstrate and earn that core value of respect. The corporal is the one who has the strong connection with, and provides support to, the men on the ground, but also has the permission to link up to the sergeant. That connection then goes through the ranks to the very top. As the mediator between the men and the sergeant, the corporal needs to earn the respect of those above and below him, and also show respect to those above and below him. Respect does not merely travel upwards to those further up the hierarchy, but equally travels down to those who you may have the privilege to lead, who are, after all, the aspiring leaders of tomorrow. This makes the role of corporal, or middle leadership, one of the most important.

One person who was pivotal during my time in Marines training was my section commander, Rick Wallace. He was a non-commissioned officer with the rank of corporal at the time, a wily old fox who would never ask you to do something that he wouldn't do himself. Humble and devoid of ego, I remember Rick as someone who always encouraged. It would have been easy to continually pick holes in all that we did, but Rick was an early role model for me who took the time to ensure that we knew what we were doing and why, as well as how we were going to do it. He went out of his way to make sure we were ready. It wasn't about his rank; he earned my respect through his actions. Even in a natural position of responsibility, whether in the family or in business, you still have to earn respect. Are you proactive in earning that respect or simply expecting it to flow to you? Is your respect flowing out to those around you, regardless of rank or responsibility? And how are you showing that respect? One thing that I've noticed along my journey is that the most valuable thing you have to give to someone is time. For someone like Rick, who freely gave his weekends and evenings so that we might one day reach the required standard of the green beret, it was clearly important to him that we were the best version of ourselves every single day. That time he gave to us was something I've never forgotten. Rick respected us as recruits and as human beings. We knew very little, but that wasn't going to stop him inspiring us to success.

The role of the leader

When I was going through my training as a Marine in 1987, it was quite brutal in that, if you couldn't the cut the mustard, you fell by the wayside. That approach has changed over the years, however. The programme has been brought into the twenty-first century and there is now a clear 'Teach, Coach and Mentor' way of training and leading – and it works. What that means in practice is that you stand in front of a group of Marines and teach them, you stand beside them as you coach them, and then stand just behind and guide them through their development as a mentor. Leadership has nothing to do with being in charge; it's about creating a safe environment and inspiring the people you have the privilege to lead. This is how team culture is cultivated and maintained, through leaders setting the tone and creating a safe environment for others to flourish. It clearly demonstrates the Marine way that respect is not earned through rank or position but through knowledge and actions. It's the same whether you are a parent, a sportsperson, a teacher or a top business executive – your knowledge and actions will gain you the respect you genuinely deserve.

This style of mentoring engenders a positive culture of sharing knowledge and experience, with the aim of improving yourself and others. Something that I developed over my time as a leader in the Marines was how essential it was to communicate effectively with your team and how imperative it was to build up individual relationships within that team. As a senior officer, if someone new joined our unit, even if he was a senior sergeant major with twenty years' worth of experience, then I would make the time to sit and get to know them, sharing personal anecdotes, showing a level of vulnerability and letting them know that we are one team. This proved to be vital in setting out the way we work together. I would also articulate that I had their back even if things went wrong. That offered them high levels of trust and empowerment, because they knew they were trusted to make decisions at their level. This engendered mutual respect and a spirit of trust that enhanced our overall combined effectiveness. I have found that this proves to be an effective way of leading in the longer term and that your people are more likely to go the extra mile for you if they trust and respect you. If you show trust in people then they will rarely let you down and they will offer you the best version of themselves.

One of the most powerful moments I have ever experienced that relates to leadership rising to the fore and earning that respect came about during the time I worked as part of a selected group of Royal Marines officer mentors with the Team GB women's hockey team in 2011. It was a year until the 2012 Olympic Games and their team management believed that some time spent with the Royal Marines could help them in their quest for a medal.

They came down for a week's work with us and it was soon apparent that they were a highly focused team with very clear goals. We set out various tasks that would require them to demonstrate different skills such as communication or teamwork alongside physical and mental demands that would challenge their leadership and resilience. We were certainly not in the business of trying to turn them into Marines, but, just as we do with our Marines, we put them in an unusual and uncomfortable environment, slightly out of their comfort zone, before adding a little pressure to see how they responded. A lot of self-learning takes place in these moments. I have seen many people and teams across multiple industries fold when the pressure is on, and in particular relationships between team members can break down. In some circumstances, especially under pressure, respect can be tossed aside amid other mixed emotions and desires; strong emotions such as frustration and anger can override it. But that is where such training can be so powerful – you experience these emotions together, learn how to process them *respectfully*, and come out the other side better for it.

The Marines attempt to train as close to reality as possible, so there is a sense of being in the environment you may well face. In some situations, whether in the Arctic, desert, jungle or mountain ranges, there will be moments where you have to act rapidly, coming up with the best plan possible based on the information around you. Each training scenario is designed to bring the team together, to broaden their horizons and to provoke deep thought and deliberation. This type of training allows for many by-products and benefits. You have been through a unique shared experience with others that you can draw from later as a team, and you now have that knowledge that you can come together when the

pressure is on. This is something that we attempted to replicate with the hockey team, under their inspirational captain,
Kate Richardson-Walsh, to bring them closer together so
that they were more aware of the capabilities and skillsets
of the members of their squad. It was designed to be a week
of enlightenment, with respect and other key values at the
forefront of the teams' shared learning.

Kate struck me immediately as someone who was
extremely proud to lead her national team. As captain she was
totally engaged with us, continually searching for any tips on
how she could lead her team better. Kate came across to me
as a humble and authentic person, with a growth mindset and
work ethic that quickly earned my respect.

In the Marines, we put the men through progressive training, with each challenge building on the last. With Team
GB Hockey, we followed the same method. Each session was
designed so that they went through the task in small groups
before reflecting back on any shared lessons and talking about
them with the wider team. When you stretch yourself beyond
your comfort zone in an unfamiliar setting, you understand
more about yourself, your team and their capabilities in how
they react under different circumstances; watching individuals
within the team rise to each challenge builds mutual respect.
Feedback and facilitation are critical – as is the importance of
allowing each team member, no matter how inexperienced
or junior, to speak and share what they have learnt at each
stage. A listening leader is a good leader, and being respectful
enough to take interest in the views of others and allow an
open forum for discussion is a highly effective way to gain
respect and to maximise learning across any group.

While we engaged with the team and drove self-reflection sessions, it was Kate who approached me several times during the course of the week in her quest to be a more effective leader. Her proactive approach allowed me to engage with her personally and authentically and to share the leadership lessons that had been passed on to me over the years. These included operational lessons such as commanding from the front, leading by example and staying calm under pressure. I reinforced that a successful leader will set a positive tone and respectful environment in which others will thrive, and that such leaders connect with and inspire others to give the very best of themselves every single day. Good leaders take less of the credit and more of the blame, thereby protecting their people and ensuring that they get rewarded for their own good performance. This builds the leader's respect for their people and the people's respect for their leader. This is a two-way experience, where both leaders and people must connect, with a clear and mutual purpose, while striving towards common goals. Leadership is a lifelong learning process with respect at its core.

Kate understood that the respect that is earned and shared between individuals and their leader can be a key factor is optimising the performance of any team; whether that was on the hockey pitch or in wider life. Each person is encouraged by the leader to recognise their own individual traits, to respect the traits of others, and to combine these together to create a unique, diverse and strong team. This encourages each member to respect one another for what skillsets they are able to bring to any task, thereby acknowledging the power of such diversity and breadth.

An example of the military-style challenges that we set Team GB Hockey included the following scenario: they are a covert Special Forces unit and they have to move the team and their equipment from one area to another, navigating across rough ground through underwater and complex obstacles, requiring them to be innovative in how they plan, communicate and complete such a mission. A leader is nominated and then roles are handed out by them, each one critical to the success of the mission; just as in a hockey match, or any team for that matter, each person has a role they have to execute well in order to achieve the group's shared goal. Each member was therefore reliant on one another, with the success of the mission at stake.

We could see how much the GB hockey team were enjoying the challenges, but from early on we had noticed that there was something not quite as it should be. While they worked hard to complete their tasks, every time it came to lunch or a break, it was obvious that cliques had formed, as the same people always sat down together in the same groups every day. Through observation and conversation, we deduced that Kate's leadership was being challenged in some way, and there were two clear groups that were forming within this team. We believed that there was somebody else who also had aspirations to be the captain going into the London 2012 Olympics. All too aware that a divided house will fall, we felt we had to try in some way to address this, and we had devised the perfect opportunity to unite them all and bring them together.

On the Friday, we had put together a tough and challenging final exercise lasting three hours that took the women to their physical and mental limits. It had been a tough week up to this point, as they had already completed everything that we had thrown at them, from underwater challenges to feats of skill and endurance requiring strength and mental fortitude. However, the culmination of all that we had done with them was to be tested on the final day. We hoped that what we had teased out of them during the week would be brought together and they would rally behind a common vision, a united purpose, and transfer that into high performance with the will of champions.

They were divided into two teams, one under the leadership of Kate – who I must say is one of the most inspirational people I have ever had the pleasure of knowing, and we are still friends to this day. Whilst already fatigued from the week's activities, each team had to cover the heathland of Woodbury Common, where the Marine recruits conduct most of their training, in as quick a time as possible, navigating under time pressure from point to point. At various checkpoints, there were obstacles, such as the infamous 'Crocodile Pit', where they had to build a rope traverse to bridge the chasm. For this the leader had to be able to plan, communicate and delegate clear tasks to each team member. It also required the ability to listen. At each checkpoint, they retrieved additional equipment such as full Jerry cans of water, and we threw in unexpected scenarios such as simulated casualties that had to be carried. We wanted to replicate that feeling when time is running out on a sports field, when you are fatigued, when the unexpected happens, and when the pressure is on to get that winning goal or simply hold on for victory. Such small margins can make the difference between champions and also-rans.

Over the course of this challenge Kate really came into her own. It was extremely rewarding for us to watch the way in which she nurtured and encouraged her team, some of whom were struggling with the physical and mental demands that we had placed on them. Kate had clearly taken in some of our key lessons and positioned herself where she could continually assess the performance of her team. Where needed, she made a change of personnel, swapping kit and equipment at various stages, thereby maximising their output while demonstrating a knowledge of the strengths, weaknesses and skillsets of each member of the group.

Kate's style of leadership was infectious and it seemed to drive her team onwards when it was clear that many were pushing at the outer limits of their own capabilities, which is where the real learning takes place. So much growth takes place in these moments, and it is a place where you can close the gap on your competitors from behind or increase the lead if you are ahead. This is a tough thing to do. Kate had understood that *this* was the reason they had come down to visit the Marines. After an incredible effort, both teams raced towards the finish line. They had given everything, yet Kate was still demanding more of her team: 'Just keep going – we can do this!' Kate's team came into the finishing strait just ahead of the other, but, under her direction, they stopped and cheered the other team, so that they came in side by side, together as one team. Never leave a teammate behind; just like the Marines.

We had what we call a 'hot debrief' while the adrenaline was still pumping and the experience was fresh in their minds. Reflection and feedback are very important, and instead of asking Kate how she felt the teams had performed, we asked the group to comment on the task and Kate's style of leadership throughout. To my amazement, the girl who was being possibly touted as the next GB captain, possibly in time for the Olympics, stood up and stated, 'Kate is our leader. She has been inspirational as the captain of England for many years. She is a role model for us all and we all want to be like Kate. She has to be the one to lead us to a medal at the Olympic Games.' The respect that Kate had earned from her team through her performance was there for all to see. It was extremely powerful.

They all stood up and started hugging each other and we just disappeared into the shadows. Leadership and personal values are often tested to the max, especially when under duress and extremes of pressure. This wasn't just about Kate, however; it was about uniting the team that she had the privilege to lead, and she knew it. She had earned their respect, and it was clear that she respected them too.

Thankfully, the story didn't end there. Those bonds of respect, camaraderie and high-performance values not only shone at London 2012, but four years later as well. During the first match of the London Games against Japan, Kate had her jaw smashed with a hockey stick. That was meant to be the end of her tournament, but after undergoing surgery she refused to sit on the sidelines and returned with a wired-up jaw and protective facemask to help drive her team to a bronze medal, the first for GB Hockey in twenty years. Kate was never going to give up on her team, no matter what. Now that is Commando spirit at its best. A true inspiration.

Four years later, I was in buckets of tears watching Kate

on TV lead the GB women to an Olympic gold medal in Rio 2016 with a dramatic victory over the Netherlands on penalties. It was amazing to watch them celebrate. I knew how much that gold medal meant to them.

Kate was then selected to be the Team GB flag-bearer at the closing ceremony, which just goes to show, once earned, genuine respect can go a very long way!

Investing in the leaders of tomorrow

Marines, even at the junior levels, are heavily invested in over a period of years, and are given training, tools and strategies so that they can become effective leaders further along in their careers. This empowerment is critical and the Marines realise how important it is to provide experienced role models for less experienced recruits – people who can guide and nurture them at every stage of their development. As a result, the young Marines immediately begin to feel a sense of belonging and have someone on hand to help them understand their new identity and the culture and values that shape it.

Investment in junior leadership can be a game-changer in wider society. Conferring the responsibility of leadership on younger people means they become invested in their society. So, for example, the culture of a school is not just determined by the headteacher and teachers, but also by the pupils. And the pupils themselves then go on to instil this in each subsequent intake; the new boys and girls immediately get a sense of what is expected in the school and they receive this understanding from their peers in the school years above them. Suddenly role models are not to be found in the staff room, but on the playground and in the classrooms.

We need to invest in young leaders in schools and the wider community, so that the respect that has been lost can be revived. That goes for respect for the elderly, respect for authority, respect for where you live – the sense of mutual respect that is ingrained in the Marines and makes that organisation so effective is the same core value that we are in desperate need of today in wider society.

This will require not just investment in our youth of today, but a clear programme of junior leadership identification, where young people have the opportunity to nurture their potential as the community leaders of tomorrow. We must attempt to bridge the divide between youth and our nation's leaders, where each respects each other, where deep and lasting connections can be made that enhance society and not damage it. As discussed, the role of the corporal, or middle leader, is crucial in this.

One of the clear areas where there has been a breakdown in mutual respect is found in large sections of the Black community and how they view the police. The development of the Black Lives Matter movement has given a clear indication of how aggrieved many feel. The flow of respect that I have talked about has become toxic in certain areas of our society, and the question is often asked: why do so many young people have a lack of respect?

Many kids lack confidence, they lack education, a mistrust of people they don't know develops and so they end up walking around with pit bulls and knives and the only role models they can see are those getting rich quick by disrespecting others, stealing and selling drugs. That is a culture of disrespect and it's a way of living that can quickly become normalised.

Such destructive behaviour can only be broken by a culture of respect, and this is where the role of the junior leader is so critical. They not only bridge the gap between our youth and natural leaders (such as teachers, parents and youth officers), but they are also empowered to challenge these natural leaders if they feel that they have done something that has eroded that respect. They need to see that the natural leaders in their areas care and respect them and that disrespect is not tolerated. So, it needs to be two-way relationship, where young men and women are listened to and invested in to become the young corporals in their area, in their family. School is a great starting point, but also it has to be seen in the home, in the community centre and on the street corner.

The role of community policing is a hot topic that has to be addressed. Young people may ask: how can you expect me to trust the police when I feel harassed? That is only going to change through effective communication, education and by building a mutual respect based on trust.

So, a young person should feel empowered to ask police, in a calm and measured way: 'Why am I being stopped?' and 'What would you like me to do?' And the police in turn should meet with youth leaders and explain why they carry out stop and search and how they expect a person to act in that scenario. This exchange of perspectives is crucial to building mutual respect. That's community support, that's building mutual respect and trust, and taking a step towards developing a positive new culture in the community. It's not leadership by rank or authority which says, 'I'm the boss, I have the power and you just do what you're told.' If that's the approach of any leader or person in authority, no matter what the environment, then they're probably in the wrong job.

My deep respect for the men in the green beret gave me a new direction in life. They offered me a new way of thinking and I bought into that new culture because they believed in me, they respected me and they saw potential in me when I didn't even see it in myself. That belief is what young people need today. It's naturally the case that teenagers cannot see their full potential, they are unable to, or prevented from seeing, what they could become because they are having to deal with so much as they grow up. Twenty-first-century life places more pressure on the young than ever before. So, it is up to adults to make the time to help them create a vision and by doing so offer them respect for the great untapped potential inside them. I felt the effects of this a couple of weeks into my Marines training. I felt as though the Peckham shackles had been lifted off me at last and I could be who I wanted to be. I love south London but, in that environment, I had allowed myself to be restricted to a narrow mindset of what life could be like for me – and it was reflected in the belief, or lack of, from some of those around me who thought I could never become a Royal Marines Commando. I had to throw off that negative mindset to unlock my full potential and self-respect, and that's a lesson for everyone, young or old.

How powerful it would be for society if everyone reading this, whatever their situation may be, grabbed hold of this value of respect and worked at making it grow within their immediate group. One particularly powerful example of where this can be applied is within the family unit. Just as in the Marines, where respect is clearly evident between the men who don the green beret, there needs to be a natural flow of respect from parent to child and back around again. The corporals in the family unit could easily be identified as, for example, those older siblings who, like the corporals in the Marines, help the younger children understand the boundaries and behaviours of what is expected in the home and demonstrate what can be achieved by hard work at school, while also engaging in a mature way with their parents. Within that respectful unit there will naturally flourish confidence and belief. That can be a game-changer for a family and for the expectations of young people, who will naturally feel a greater sense of identity and belonging because of the mutual values and respect within the family unit. The culture in the home organically changes for the better when that mutual respect is flowing, and that then spills out in a positive manner to the rest of the community and in wider society.

It's the same in business. The standards are laid down by the senior leaders and the managers below them so that every member of the workforce understands what is expected in the working environment. As with the Marines and the family unit, out of this mutual understanding will evolve a sense of identity and belonging, which enables and empowers everyone to thrive. And when adversity comes, there is a feeling of togetherness and respect for each other to get through it because everyone is personally invested and feels a connection with the business and their colleagues.

When I worked with the England football team, this was something that the manager Gareth Southgate was very keen to see develop. He wanted to improve the junior leadership (the corporals if you like) and to incorporate leaders at every level to bind the team together. So, Harry Kane, Jordan Henderson and others were given key leadership roles and they linked up to the management while also dealing with issues to support their teammates. That meant issues were brought to them and dealt with in the right way, they were nipped in the bud early and not allowed to fester and worsen. Like Marine NCOs, these players understood the importance of being the arbiter of the standards and, through their actions, they represented their team as authentic leaders while respecting the privilege that came with such a position.

There is nothing worse than low morale and toxicity in any team, whether that is a group of Marines on operational duty or a sports team preparing to try to win a World Cup. To protect morale, you need the right people with the right mindset led by the right leaders, promoting an environment with mutual respect at its core.

Personal responsibility goes hand in hand with mutual respect. Taking ownership of not just your own performance but also the performance of others is intertwined with the way in which you respect yourself and others. By taking ownership and therefore responsibility of the destiny of others in a selfless way, you are making a statement that you will accept charge of your duty as a trusted member of a group. You can't demand respect and yet not be prepared to take personal responsibility for your actions. The blame game and excuse-making won't cut it in a culture of respect – whether that's the leader who never listens, the parent who has gambled away the holiday money or the boss who in a moment of anger has belittled a colleague.

A culture of mutual respect has no room for selfishness. In the Marines, we call being selfish 'being Jack'. It quite simply cannot be tolerated – and the stakes are high. As Marines we can be deployed at any moment to an extreme operational environment where you have to trust your team at every juncture. A failure of trust and respect will result in a reduced overall effectiveness that could erode morale and set a toxic environment where someone could become severely injured or even killed. On occasion, when you haven't slept for several days in a row, you always welcome the opportunity to take a period of rest while sentries stand guard. One of the worst crimes in the Marines is to fall asleep on duty. You have been trusted and empowered with the safety of your sleeping comrades in an environment where failure to respect that huge personal responsibility will result in catastrophe.

The green beret, as I've said, is the ultimate badge of acceptance, honour and mutual respect. Only those who have earned it truly know what it stands for. It defines us, drives us and unites us. The DNA of a Marine sees past colour or creed, and its acceptance of such diversity, and its tolerance towards others, is indicative of the respect that is universally shown in our Corps. The only time I ever noticed I had a different skin colour to most Marines was when I looked in the mirror to have a shave. It's why I stayed for over thirty years.

Our society needs to have that same respect – one that has trust and empowerment at its core. Whether you aim to build respect in a relationship, or earn respect at work or school, I've found that it is critical to keep your promises to others and to see things through when others rely on you. Being considerate and discreet, helping other people in tough times, and going the extra mile in everything that you do, certainly goes a long way towards earning the respect that you may yearn for. It's not something you can fake; you have to *want* to do it, and you have to be prepared to work for it. Give it a try, and you'll find that not only will you quickly go up in the estimation of other people, you'll also have more respect for yourself.

CHAPTER 1: RESPECT
LESSON SUMMARY

Remember ...

* Respect is *not* earned through rank or position, but through what you do and how you do it – every single day.
* Respect is blind to colour, gender, creed or age.
* If you earn a reputation and respect for getting the small things right, the big things will soon follow.

Step 1 – WHAT is respect?

Respect is the deep admiration that someone feels for you, or you have for someone because of their abilities, qualities, or achievements. There are three elements to respect: firstly, respect for yourself; secondly, respect for others; and thirdly, the respect others have for you. Mutual respect is the goal.

Step 2 – WHY is respect is important?

Showing respect means that you accept a person for who they are and what they do, even if they think differently to you or if you disagree with them. This works both ways. Respect in your relationships builds feelings of trust, security and camaraderie. You aren't born with respect; it is something that you earn, learn and develop as part of your journey.

Step 3 – HOW to build and incorporate respect into your life.

- Surround yourself with people who you respect and who respect you.
- Let your actions speak louder than words.
- Be open to new ideas and different ways of thinking.
- Inspire people and invest your time and energy into them.
- Keep all of your promises.

CHAPTER 2

Overcoming

Definition: Your ability to surmount life's obstacles, problems or difficulties.

Refusing to give in to fear

Nothing quite focuses the mind like being told you have a 20 per cent chance of surviving the day. I was about to embark on the most memorable operation of my military career, spearheading the invasion of Iraq, when one of the senior officers felt he had to tell me just what my troops and I were facing. It was the one and only true do-or-die mission I was involved in.

It was 2003 and the world had run out of patience with Saddam Hussein and his threat of chemical weapons. Prime Minister Tony Blair and US President George Bush ordered the invasion and it would be the 150 men of 'Charlie' Company in 40 Commando Royal Marines, based in Taunton, who would spearhead the mission.

Some 330,000 Coalition troops were now amassing across the Kuwaiti border on ships, awaiting orders for the invasion. 40 Commando had positioned themselves on the border at Camp Commando, where we sat for five days in the worst sandstorm the region had seen for decades. Life was simple here; we shared the desert with scorpions, deadly snakes and camels, and it was roasting hot when the sandstorm subsided. Deep 'trench latrines' were dug into the desert with a plank that you sat on and hung your backside over. It was common for ten blokes so be sat there together, passing the time of day. I remember while waiting in the desert that a 'scud missile chemical attack' alarm went off. We all, naturally, had to take cover and get into the first and closest trench or dugout that we could and rapidly don our respirator gas masks in case of chemical attack. The lads caught out on the latrine at the time only had one route out; to launch themselves into the two-metre-deep trench of human waste. When the false alarm was sounded, they emerged from the pit covered in 100 blokes' worth of dung – which was rather ripe in 50+ degrees Celsius! Some of that famous Marines 'cheerfulness in the face of adversity' was certainly called for as they dragged themselves out of the shit pit, much to the amusement of everyone else.

The aim of the knife-edge assault was to take control of the Iraqi oil infrastructure through a Manifold and Metering Station (MMS), which was the main point of control for the flow of oil from Iraq into the Northern Arabian Gulf.

Working alongside US Navy Seal teams, we had to transport an analyst to the MMS, where they could plug into the system and direct the flow of oil away from the Iraqis and into Coalition hands. That would set up the success of the whole conflict. It was about avoiding a similar ecological disaster to that which had happened in the Gulf War of 1991, when Saddam set the oil fields on fire.

The only problem was that the Iraqis knew we were coming. They were ready for us; their land, sea and air defences were set, and I knew we were going into a mission that would go down in history. There is no doubt that in the hours before boarding the aircraft it would have been easy to have been gripped by fear, particularly having been told the low chance of success.

This was obvious, given that we had three large Chinook helicopters going into the Al-Faw peninsula which is on Iraq's southernmost tip and an obvious attack point. We had forty-four men on board each craft, including an analyst, because if the first one got blown out of the sky – the one I was in – then the second and third could complete the task, as they were made up of the same unit. The ideal situation would be for all three troops of forty-four to make it through, but, just in case, there would be three bites at the apple. We were determined to make sure it only required one.

As we stood together in a huddle, preparing for our mission, I pulled the lads in and told my brothers that nobody was going to be left behind in a sandy shallow grave in Iraq. It was important to say it out loud, and we all gave each other that steely look in the eye as if to acknowledge our pledge to each other. I was convinced we would execute the plan laid out for us. That pledge to each other, that nobody would be left behind, seemed to cut the tension, and as we boarded the Chinook, I didn't see fear or apprehension in the men's eyes – just a real focus of intent. We had trained hard, we had honed our skills and left no stone unturned. We were physically and mentally ready, and we knew it.

There will be critical moments in life when you have to take a deliberate, and often difficult, decision to overcome – whether that's overcoming a practical obstacle, a mental hurdle or your own fear. Standing waiting to board the Chinook was our moment for overcoming fear. As a senior commander, I had to decide how best to manage that fear within our team. I didn't share with my men that we only had a 20 per cent chance of survival. That seemed pointless and would only have increased the chance of fear gripping the ranks. I didn't want the 20 per cent statistic to take hold because it would only breed anxiety, and the 'white noise' of fear would only distract us from our purpose. Instead, we focused on how well prepared we were and on the fortitude and skills we possessed to complete our mission. In my experience, fear can be overcome through a combination of confidence and excitement.

On that particular day, it was easier because we were not alone. Our troop had bonded strongly and we knew that we had each other's backs. No doubt about it. We could also feel our Royal Marine forefathers watching us and knew we were about to make history. We were ready to stand together, united to the end. I would have done anything for my boys. I would have put my life on the line for any of them, and I knew that they would do the same for me. It's a unique and special bond with an unbreakable level of trust that goes beyond anything that I can describe in words. It is the epitome of the Commando spirit; courage, sacrifice, camaraderie and selflessness. This was to be the most profound and pivotal moment, one which was likely to define the rest of our lives. As a senior commander on the ground, it was such a privilege to lead these men into battle. And I was so proud to stand among these fine men, to be a part of this special 'band of brothers'.

As we took off, this signalled the start of the Iraq War, as we were privileged to be *the* theatre entry troops, 'first on the ground' out of almost a third of a million coalition military personnel. With an excess of 150lbs of equipment each on our backs, there was standing room only on the Chinook as the men of 'Charlie' Company flew in at low level, trying to maintain our balance as the masterful pilots swayed left and right, up and down, avoiding the dangerous low power lines. We soon left Kuwaiti airspace, transiting over Bubiyan Island and across the Northern Arabian Gulf toward the Iraqi coast.

The greatest pleasure or sense of achievement is often on the other side of your darkest fears, and at four o'clock in the morning the RAF pilots landed us in the exact spot we needed to be in. The Iraqis had expected us to come in by fast amphibious craft, but we had flown over them, despite their anti-aircraft assaults – their tracer bullets lighting up the night sky. While in the air, news came through my headset that a helicopter had crashed in a different area as part of the Marines entry operation. I was saddened but couldn't focus on that now. We had a job to do. It would have been easy to become distracted by this bad news, wondering if you knew anyone aboard, and allowing such a tragedy to affect your thinking. Of course, there would be time for deeper reflection and grief later on, but this was not the time for that. At times, it is paramount to eliminate the white noise and focus only on those things that you can control. Focusing on what we *can't* control often takes our energy and attention from what we *can*. Maintaining a deep and clear focus on what matters is a technique that you will find useful, but it takes discipline and practice.

A glimpse of land became visible from the open tailgate and I knew we were now over Iraq. I kept reminding myself that the training, planning and preparation was all done. I just had to keep focused, expect the unexpected and, above all else, look after the lads.

Having landed safely, there was a deathly silence as the helicopters flew away into the night. We got into our defensive circle, my corporals came to me to confirm we were all ready to go, and one of them, Marty Culley, a great Marine NCO with a dry and quirky sense of humour, decided to start singing in my ear that Bjork song 'It's Oh So Quiet'. As if by magic, when he got to the line 'The sky up above zing boom is caving in', American A10 Interceptors and B52 spectre gunships had already started taking out enemy positions 100 metres either side of us. I have to admit, with the Yanks backing us up, I thought our chances of survival just dropped to 10 per cent! But, in fairness, the US fighters had already proved themselves extremely accurate, having previously taken out most of the Iraqi resistance around us in quick order.

It was also time to go. We had to take control of five objectives and secure the pipelines, and as we made our way into combat there were firefights either side of us, thankfully taking out any remaining enemy. A few hours later, in over 50-degree heat, the unit had taken all its objectives and 150 prisoners, and not suffered one single fatality. The oil was under the control of the Coalition forces and, for its efforts, 40 Commando Royal Marines were awarded a Battle Honour. We had defied fear and overcome the odds, through a combination of focus and determination. We had overcome in the most extreme environment under the most intense pressure. Being one of the commanders on the ground for that operation was one of the proudest moments of my career. The credit goes to the young Marines on the ground who never once wavered or shirked from their responsibilities. Overcoming fear is something to be extremely proud of – and key to this is that ability to remove the white noise, to focus on what is within your control and perform to the best of your ability whilst under extreme pressure. In the face of such focus, fear is forced to take a back seat, leaving you in the driving seat.

Identifying your obstacle and using focus to overcome

During our lives we come across obstacles that seem more like permanent barriers that stop us in our tracks. The starting point is to view them as something that can be overcome, reframing the obstacle as a challenge that may stretch you, but which is within your grasp. The next step is to identify the 'how', the means by which you will tackle this challenge. The vehicle for change in my life, which helped me overcome my own obstacles, was the Royal Marines. You will have your own vehicle. It could be anything from the course that you've always wanted to do at the local college, to that job you want to try for, to the exams you need to strive for.

The concept of 'overcoming' is repeated often throughout Marine training. While situations may vary, we can apply the same rules and values to a huge array of different scenarios across every industry, whether on the sports field or in the office, the home or classroom. In life we all have enemies that rear their heads ready to overwhelm us – fear, loss, hardship, bitterness, the bully, the past, present and the future. These enemies can only be overcome with a relentless focus on the ultimate goal, putting this ahead of the obstacles, heartache or fear of failure: that relationship you have to move on from, the financial blow you have suffered, that bully in the workplace – maybe even just getting through another day.

Often it's the thoughts that we have, the way we build up a problem in our heads, that paralyse us. If we find ourselves simply focusing on the problems, we will only see the darkness that surrounds us, not the possibility for light. We all need some light to aim towards in our lives. So, define your goal, narrow your focus, maintain a positive mindset and believe that you *will* overcome – no matter what.

In order to overcome, it's necessary to keep focus. Ask yourself: what's your mission today? When you push away all the white noise, what is your goal? When that is established, you must plan how that will be achieved, and you must follow that plan through. Detailed, meticulous planning and the discipline of seeing that plan through to its conclusion *will* see you overcome any situation. Especially when things go wrong – this is when it is even more important to go back to your plan and narrow your focus.

It might be that you have to adjust your plan of action as you go, so maintaining a level of flexibility is also key. Expect the unexpected, and be prepared to deal with the inevitable curveballs that life throws at you from time to time. The Marines say that 'no plan survives contact with the enemy', and this is true, but you cannot drive forwards without knowing which direction you are heading and why, so it is important to start out with a plan but be willing to adapt as you work through it. Keep a focus on your end-goal and you won't go far wrong. I know it works in the Royal Marines, and it will work for you too.

Whether it is on the field of combat, in the sports arena or in life, the principle of overcoming remains the same. Taking a moment to find a resolute calmness to focus on what is to be done to achieve your goal is crucial. Build these moments of reflection and calm into your plan before you set out and use them to congratulate yourself on how far you have come, reassess your route forward, and centre your goal. The enemy that is seeking to bring you down will be defeated if you continue to defiantly focus on the place you want to get to. Understanding your desired destination is key – and so is the support of others as you strive towards what may appear to be an impossible dream.

Overcoming as a team

Overcoming is not something that you should naturally do alone. The people around you can be hugely important. Working as a team, trusting each other and offering mutual support are so helpful in seeking to achieve goals in life and can help to galvanise your spirit as you summon the will to go on when the way ahead looks bleak. Seeking help is not a sign of weakness. In fact, from my experiences in life, war, sport and business, I see more and more that it takes courage and is a sign of strength to accept support from the people who care. Often, going it alone will weaken your position; as a united team you can remain resilient, adaptable and crucial to the lives of those around you.

It was this team mentality of overcoming adversity together that we brought to the England football team when manager Gareth Southgate came to us a year out from the 2018 World Cup finals in Russia. I had already done some work with the England rugby team ahead of their World Cup success of 2003, and it was one of the coaches from Sir Clive Woodward's backroom staff, who now worked for England FA and who had been to the Lympstone Marine training camp, who suggested it might be good for the footballers too.

One of our officers travelled to the home of England at St George's Park in Burton-on-Trent and burst into the briefing room where all the team were waiting. It was kept a secret from both players and staff, who were stunned to hear that they would be coming down to Lympstone to train alongside the Marines. They had their phones and watches confiscated on the spot and put in a box for safekeeping. There would be no unofficial photos, cameras or phones, and the team could be themselves and feel safe in our presence. On arrival, they were quickly transformed from England stars into Marine trainees with green fatigues and camouflage cream. They were unrecognisable, and we had achieved the first aim: to remove their identity as football superstars. As Marines, we never make a big fuss around celebrities anyway, and I got the sense that the England team liked it this way.

Gareth and I got on like a house on fire straight away. What an absolute gentleman he is. He listens intently to what you say and makes you feel instantly at ease; two impressive qualities for any leader to aspire to. Not every leader of his stature has these qualities. We spoke about family and our love for football, and he realised that I was a huge England fan, and that I would do everything in my power to help 'our' England team to grow. We discussed what he wanted to get out of the weekend, with team cohesion and leadership growth being high on his agenda.

It's no secret that the England football team have failed in recent years, unable to win a major trophy since 1966, often due to being paralysed through fear of failure. Having got to know him well, it's no surprise to me that under Gareth's leadership the national team has gone to a World Cup semi-final, in 2018, and a European Championship final, in 2021, where they came so close to glory. Gareth is fully aware of how difficult it is to replicate the pressure of key moments in game play, such as the so-called dreaded penalties, but he was also cognisant that the team could learn different but valuable lessons by placing them in unusual, pressurised scenarios outside of football. You can find out so much about yourself and about those around you by pushing your limits in ways you never thought possible.

It's often easy to shine in your own environment, where you feel comfortable, but equally that can be a place where you rarely feel tested and stretched. By challenging yourself in different ways – outside of your comfort zone – you will find that a huge amount of growth takes place. Stepping into the unknown, taking on that new challenge in your life, you encounter obstacles you may never have seen before, but then you learn how to overcome them despite the huge expectations and overwhelming pressure to succeed. Overcoming in one area will empower you with the confidence to overcome and achieve in another different environment. The belief that you can overcome and find a way to achieve a goal becomes stronger and stronger to the point you believe you can overcome anything.

It has always been a challenge for England managers to inspire players from different club teams to be teammates rather than the opponents they are for the rest of the season. I had heard the stories of club cliques forming in the England set-up, and how that was damaging to team unity. I had also heard that some of the previous players stopped looking forward to being selected and playing for England and valued their club more than representing their nation, which I found mind-boggling. In my view, the pride of representing your nation at anything comes with great responsibility and should be the pinnacle of anyone's career. I felt that we could really help them to grow in many areas, such as patriotic pride, resilience, ownership and being composed under pressure. As I always say, 'The greatest teams perform at their best when the pressure is at its highest.'

Early the next day, after a field breakfast, we had a surprise in store for them. I hid with six Royal Marines physical training instructors at the start of that day's challenge, and we all jumped out and scared the crap out of them when they arrived. We were about to embark on the world-famous Royal Marines endurance course, one of our final Commando tests, which comprises two and a half miles of underwater obstacles and submerged tunnels with names such as the Crocodile Pit, Peters Pool and the Smartie Tubes. They were split into groups for the course, and each group had to complete the course as part of a team. 'We go as fast as the slowest man or woman,' I told them. Marines recruits in training do this with their full weight of kit, so a bit of perspective was offered to the players as to how 'easy' they had it in the June sunshine – in stark contrast to our trainees, who do it in all weather conditions, sometimes breaking the ice for a sustained sub-zero underwater experience.

My group included, among others, Harry Kane and Gareth. As we set off, we ran through the mud, up the hills, crawled through the pitch-black underwater tunnels and headed down to the 'Sheep Dip'. This consists of a fully submerged, long, narrow tunnel that requires your teammate to push you 'down and in'. Once inside, you cannot move at all; you certainly couldn't swim out of the tunnel, and you are totally reliant on the teammate at the other end of the tunnel to pull you out. If the person at the end doesn't pull you through, then, no two ways about it, you will drown. This is the obstacle where we often have 'refusals', even among

Marine recruits. The expectation and pressure to perform in this alien environment is mostly self-induced, and it is very common for feelings of apprehension to be overwhelming for the participant.

As we approached the Sheep Dip, I heard some mumblings in the background. I recognised this sound and knew it to be the murmurs of self-doubt starting to creep through the group. This was actually a good thing – and was exactly the type of experience under pressure that Gareth had wanted the team to tackle.

I had tactically placed myself at the receiving end and, as Gareth led in the front group, he was first man in the tunnel. After he was pulled out safely by me on the other side, several others went through, but there was a small group of players hovering at the back. Jermain Defoe, or JD – a smashing fella – was one of them . . .

I could see his concern and I knew that the enemy of fear can swiftly spread to others and consume the group. There were already several members who were looking to JD for motivation and I knew that, with him being one of the senior players, we had to get him through otherwise the fear would suffocate the rest of the group. Peer pressure is an emotional state that manifests in many ways; in this case, the obligation to do something you might usually not because others are watching you. Your head is saying NO but your heart is saying YES. Peer pressure can have a negative or positive effect, depending on the situation you find yourself in. The first step to ensuring it's used positively is in recognising it, and then taking charge of it.

JD is a leader, and others look up to him, so it was

important for him to conquer his trepidation. I asked him to look me in the eye and I asked him, 'Do you trust me?' JD instantly replied, 'Yes, I do, Scotty.' 'Well, then,' I said, 'what you need to do is to put your life in my hands. I promise that I won't let you down.' It was one of those special bonding moments, a shared experience that I won't forget.

In that instant, JD went for it, and not only faced his fear but overcame it. I was so proud of him and the others too. What JD said when I pulled him out the other end of the Sheep Dip was a key moment not only for his personal development but also the team's evolution. 'That pressure was like taking a penalty at the World Cup,' he said, and when I heard that, I knew the Marines' spirit of overcoming was now going to run through the entire England squad. This was real teamwork working to overcome fear. Find someone who can back you like that and it's a huge benefit when things don't go to plan or when life enters a dark place.

A few days after England left the Marine Camp, I got a call to say that Gareth had invited me and one other Marines officer up to Scotland for their crucial World Cup qualifier at Hampden Park at the weekend. England were in top spot of the qualifying group, but Scotland had everything to play for – if they didn't win, it would be almost impossible for them to get to Russia. There was a lot riding on this match, and both teams knew it.

I'd been to dozens of England games over the years, but I had never been to one against the 'auld enemy', so I was very excited. As we arrived at the team hotel, Gareth told us that the team were about to have their pre-match food and that we should go in first as a surprise for the players, because they didn't know we were coming to support them. We burst in, and all the team jumped up and crowded round with hugs and handshakes. It felt wonderful to be greeted so warmly by the lads.

It was Harry Kane's first match as England captain, and I felt very privileged to be able to break away and spend some time with him before the match talking about my leadership experiences and some of the leadership lessons I had learnt over my thirty years in command. While the majority of what we spoke about remains between us, I did say to him that, as a leader, people will look to you for guidance and direction and that the test of real leadership is what you do to inspire your team when things aren't going to plan. I said to Harry that while everything might go smoothly today, there would be times when they wouldn't, and asked what he would do when such moments arose. Would he be ready to overcome, to make sure his team stood up and were counted? Or would they fold, like some other teams wearing the three lions had done in the past?

It felt like every Scotsman in the land was out that day, swigging beer and whisky, flashing the contents of their kilts at us and giving us the bird as we drove past on the team bus towards Hampden Park. The team ignored the antics outside, and I couldn't help but feel that it was a very similar feeling to being deployed to a foreign land on hostile territory with my Marines.

As we approached kick-off, we were asked to stand outside the England changing room, with our green berets on, and we saluted our new England captain Harry Kane and the England team as they emerged into the tunnel. As we went out, I asked where they wanted us to sit. To be honest, I was expecting to sit in the stands somewhere. But no – not today. I was stunned when they asked us to join the manager, staff and players sitting on the England bench. That was an awesome experience and such a privilege.

Little did I know that the moment of critical leadership I had talked about with Harry was about to come in his first match as captain. With seven minutes remaining, it seemed England were cruising to a 1-0 win, with a great goal from the brilliant Alex Oxlade-Chamberlain. But then the Scotland striker Leigh Griffiths, incredibly, scored two fantastic free kicks in quick succession and so, with a minute of normal time remaining, Scotland were now on the way to a famous victory.

The entire crowd of 60,000 Scotland fans was going bananas and I have never heard a noise like that in a football stadium (and I'm a Millwall fan, so that really is saying something). Some fans had even broken through the security barriers and were now in our faces sticking two fingers up to everyone on the bench! This was that moment that I had been coaching Harry about only a couple of hours before. It was similar to being in the Marines when the plan has gone to pieces: we are on the brink of defeat but we have to re-set, re-focus, believe in ourselves and find a way to overcome.

I then had a moment of clarity. It felt like time stood still, and I took a step back, glanced around and assessed the situation. The clock said 90+4, and the Scotland players were in the corner still celebrating their second goal. I looked towards our new captain . . .

I have personally seen several previous England teams collapse on the pitch with their heads in their hands when on the brink of defeat, but not this lot. The body language was good, Harry was leading them, and you could see him gesturing to his men to 'stand tall', 'keep composed', reassuring them that 'our chance will come'. This was the moment at which I felt extremely positive about our chances at the World Cup. They were starting to believe and were clearly taking ownership of the situation in front of them.

It paid off. Now in injury time, Kyle Walker stole the ball from Scotland, which led to a great move and a precise cross-field pass from Raheem Sterling, who found Harry, who slotted home with the last kick of the game to snatch a vital point. 'Like the Marines, we never give in,' said Gareth in the changing room later on. As a personal bonus, Harry came over and dedicated his first goal as England captain to me for the leadership support that I had shared with him on that day.

Never say die

Often it will be the case that overcoming a small goal can blossom into mountains being conquered. One day it could the Sheep Dip, the next it could be winning a tense European Championship semi-final match. And often there is a key figure who helps make that happen. One man who got the 'overcoming' ball rolling for me and a very special group of serving and ex-Marines was former Marine Mark Scoular. Mark had joined the Metropolitan Police and rose through the ranks to the point that he was put in charge of overall security for the London 2012 Olympic Games. Mark sent out a message to all ex-Marines in the emergency services asking them to come together for a five-mile 'Speed March' run in military boots and then a drink and a chat afterwards. It was to bring the guys together so they could enjoy once again that close comradeship, and he called it Commando 999. In order to do the run, he required a physical instructor and asked me to join, which I gladly did. On the first occasion we had thirty people turn up for the speed march. Then, for the 350th anniversary of the Royal Marines in 2014, he had 350 ex-Marines lined up outside 10 Downing Street and welcomed by then Prime Minister David Cameron. At the last count, Mark's efforts have raised more than £800,000 for Royal Marines charities and enriched the lives of those former Commandos in the police, fire service and ambulance service. Then, out of that, the idea came to make an attempt on the World Speed March record. In this way, overcoming small challenges can lead us on to much bigger achievements.

Speed marching is a military skill where a team runs from one point to another across the ground in a specified time whilst carrying your kit. The 9-mile speed march is actually another one of our Commando Tests in training, where the recruits must start and finish as a group whilst retaining their ability to fight at the end. It's a good test of physical robustness and mental fortitude.

The previous world record for speed marching was held by the Army, who in 1998 completed 26.2 miles in 4 hours 19 minutes and 7 seconds. A magnificent effort and a record that had stood for many years. Some had deemed it unbreakable!

In 2012, we set out to break this world record, speed marching with a team of Royal Marines over the marathon distance. Eight men running as a squad in boots with 40lbs of kit on their back (that's eighteen 1kg bags of sugar!), and all had to finish together to register a time to beat the fourteen-year-old world record. We came up short by two minutes. It was gut-wrenching, but we knew we could overcome this disappointment. Overcoming is about persistence; it means accepting when you fall short and not letting failure make you believe that your goal cannot be achieved. It means trying again and again and again, and so, a year later, we were at the start once more. On this attempt we crossed the line in a new world record time, but the only problem was that one of our eight had not made it to the finish. With just half a mile to go, my good friend Dave Perrott, whom I had served with in Iraq, had collapsed with heat exhaustion. (It is a measure of his commitment that even while lying on his back, his arms and legs were still making forward movements!) He was taken straight to hospital and put on a drip, which is just as well, because the doctor said if we had got there twenty minutes later, he would have been dead.

At the finish line in 2013, I stood up and declared our incredible, world-record-breaking time, but had to concede to the gathered family members and friends that it would not be ratified because only seven Marines crossed the finish line instead of the full team of eight. Nevertheless, the sense of pride was overwhelming, and nothing could take that away from us. There is a power in recognising how far you have come, even if it is not what you had set out to achieve.

A couple of years later, however, some of the boys came to me and said they wanted the official world record. I had come to terms with the bitter reality that, despite such an incredible effort, we had failed, but I was ready to try again. It was only by coming to terms with our previous failures that we could go ahead and make the third and final successful attempt in 2017. Sometimes in life you must accept your failings and then use that acceptance to identify your obstacles and overcome them. Victory, as they say, is just the other side of defeat.

This time around, we looked closely at our own versions of 'why' we were doing this, 'who' we were, and 'what' this world record meant to us. What was our motivation here? What did we have to do better this time around? What had we learned? We collectively bought into a common vision, a collective goal that was unique to this special team, based on our Commando qualities, values and ethos. We got to know each other even better and this enhanced communication allowed us to share each other's lives as we became more connected. The 'carryover' benefit is that, by investing more in each other, you then become even more determined not to let your teammates down. That drives you to train harder, work harder and to prepare better. In effect, we took ownership of each other's destinies. The diet was changed to be more scientific, so the Mars bars and bananas were out and in came protein shakes and carefully planned diet and nutritional aids to carry the lads through the training and ultimately the completion of the 26.2 miles. Marathon runners talk about hitting the wall around the 18-mile mark, and when you hit that with 40lbs of kit on, it *hurts* – and you place yourself at serious risk of long-term injury or even death. Maximising nutritional potential was one of the factors that we could control, and so we made it work to our utmost advantage.

Royal Marines have purpose and resolve bred into their DNA and I never cease to be amazed by their ability to cross and push both their physical and mental pain thresholds to new, uncharted levels. That winning mindset and 'never say die' attitude is what will stand you apart from others. The rollercoaster of training, injury avoidance, diet, nutrition and recovery had to be managed alongside busy jobs and family commitments. No one said it would be easy, but we were certainly making it hard for ourselves with a daily training regime that depended on each individual sticking to the plan, largely unsupervised. We would then come together for training runs at unsociable hours in all conditions at various locations. The team trained on holidays, sacrificed dinners and honeymoons (Mark and Lisa Downie) and resisted indulgence, preparing and training like Olympic athletes.

The actual attempt set off at 4 a.m. from the Cenotaph in London. We started out strong, hitting each mile marker in good time. As we progressed, the fatigue set in and the pain of the weight burned deep into our shoulders and our minds; the lads were longing for it to stop. As we got to the final 2 miles of the marathon, some 24 miles in, everyone had given their all and they were running on empty. One of the team was really struggling and was on the verge of collapse with just half a mile left – we'd been here before! But the Marines aren't renowned for giving up, and what made the difference was the power of the collective that came together to win the day. The team were fully invested in each other's success or failure and took ownership of not just their own performance but for the performances of their teammates. It was one-in all-in!

The preparation, mental fortitude, resilience and Commando spirit required to break this record was an inspiration to behold. I've had the privilege to lead Royal Marines on theatre entry operations around the globe, and I've been chosen to represent our nation at our home Olympic Games, yet this was to be one of my proudest moments.

It is the collective power of what is truly possible that allows me to conclude that this was right up there with the greatest teams that I have ever had the privilege to lead. We crossed the finishing line in a new world record of 4 hours 16 minutes and 43 seconds. Knowing we had overcome so much to achieve something really special meant so much to every one of us – and that included Dave Perrott, who had been hit hard mentally by the fact that his collapse four years previously had meant we hadn't secured the new world record. Dave was understandably gutted and felt that he had let the whole team down, which of course he hadn't. Soon after that second attempt in 2013, I had visited Dave in hospital, and seeing his mum, wife and child confirmed to me that I had made the right decision to abandon our record for his safety. Dave could not be one of the eight in the final successful world record team, but that didn't mean he did not have a role to play. I had kept in touch with Dave throughout the intervening time and I was determined to ask him to be part of the support team; it was a sweet moment when he agreed. The determination in his DNA rose to the challenge and he proved to be a very valuable member of the team. He also exorcised those demons of our failed attempt from back in 2013. With a mile to go, Dave got out of the support van and ran the last stretch with us. It was a poignant moment. Ultimately, Dave finished his own world record from four years previous when he completed that last mile. That was a big part of our combined story as we celebrated the new world record as one team.

A TV documentary by the highly acclaimed film maker Chris Terrill was made of our incredible world record achievement. It was called 'To Hell and Back', which I believe gives a great insight into not only the mentality of those who wear the green beret, but also what overcoming is all about. In my eyes, after five years in the making, this incredible achievement of human spirit, endeavour and resilience, the determination to never give up, must be right up there with a gold medal at the Olympic Games. We had to be better than great, and we were.

As the man privileged to lead this incredible team, I had to make sure that I knew every aspect of the course. Every turn, every marker, every nook and cranny. I had run it over and over again. The great Usain Bolt sums up our thought processes with his famous words: 'As long as I'm ready on the start line, there's no stopping me!' We were ready. There would be no room for doubt, blame or excuses in this final attempt because all the boxes were ticked and when we crossed the line it was courage, determination and unity at its optimum level that prevailed. The feeling of crossing the line together as world record holders was simply wonderful and a five-year dream come true.

In civilian life, I have learned that people are much more capable than they give themselves credit for. The first step to realising that is putting yourself in these vulnerable situations, raising your head above the parapet without knowing what the outcome will be. You *might* fail, but you might succeed, and whatever the outcome, you will have moved yourself further towards overcoming your obstacles. Building resilience through adversity will increase your capacity to perform better. You will never fully appreciate your limits unless you stretch yourself by taking yourself out of your comfort zone. It's how we grow. We identify our limits by embracing our failures, then we find ways to overcome these and raise the bar, thereby continually striving for improvement in all that we do.

Each failure in life is just a stepping-stone towards eventual success, to overcoming, to achieving your own gold medal in life, and with the Marine spirit, that's exactly what you can do.

CHAPTER 2: OVERCOMING LESSON SUMMARY

Remember . . .

+ Define your goal, narrow your focus, maintain a positive mindset and you *will* overcome.
+ Don't become paralysed by fear of failure. Remove the 'white noise' of fear from your life enabling you to focus on your goal.
+ Learn from your mistakes and just keep going.

Step 1 – WHAT is overcoming?

Overcoming is a state of mind enabling you to prevail against adversity, fear and challenges. You can use this skill to overcome an opposition, a debilitation or temptation. When you overcome, you successfully deal with the issue, learn to take control of it and assimilate it into your life.

Step 2 – WHY is overcoming important?

Overcoming tough situations promotes personal growth in a way that is unique. Facing adversity, fear and challenges and learning how to navigate your way through them builds resilience. Knowing that you can overcome such situations, learn from your mistakes and employ your experience allows you to bounce back quickly when the going gets tough or when things don't go your way. It also lays a solid foundation for consistently better outcomes going forwards.

Step 3 – HOW to overcome in your life.

+ Know you are not alone; seek advice from people you trust if you can't see a clear way forward.
+ Define your goal, narrow your focus, maintain a positive mindset and believe that you *will* overcome – no matter what.
+ Take ownership of tough situations and make a plan to overcome.
+ Refuse to give in to fear – replace fear with excitement and confidence.
+ Never Give In: know that your greatest achievements lie just on the other side of your darkest fears.

Self-Discipline

Definition: The necessary mental strength that is required to control one's behaviours, feelings and desires.

Lying face down in a stream wasn't in the plan – but then again, neither was falling asleep while walking!

From the moment you start training as a Marines recruit you are hit right in the face with the necessity of self-discipline. And I'd like to think that for 99.9 per cent of the time I have shown that quality. But at 4 a.m., after nine days living outdoors in the wilderness with just two hours' sleep per night during Senior Command and Leadership training, the blackout came. It was pitch–black and foggy, we couldn't see our hands in front of our faces, so we had to hold on to each other's shoulders. Suddenly, however, the lad in front of me couldn't feel my hand on his shoulder anymore, and the lad behind had stopped because he had no shoulder to put his hand on. They found me in the stream, having fallen asleep while walking. All I could do was get up, slap some water on my face, have a little giggle at the situation, and then go on. Sometimes in life that's all you can do.

During Marines training you are pushed to the limit and beyond, physically and mentally. And while coping with the extreme demands made of you, you still have to, for example, gather intelligence, receive and write orders, and then command your team. From a state of physical and mental exhaustion you will be called to carry out a mission, and this will bring out the best and the worst qualities in you. You will learn about yourself – and one of the most important lessons will be what level your self-discipline is at.

I cannot stress the importance of self-discipline enough; it will enable anyone to rise to the challenges they face in life – to face down even the toughest addiction, pass those exams, lose that weight. I can almost hear you reading this and saying, 'Yeah, Scotty, that's easy for you to say, but we're not all Marines ...' But while the Marines certainly attract recruits with a tendency towards certain character traits, not every young recruit arrives with this mindset of self-discipline already built in. It's a characteristic that can be – and frequently is – learned. In fact, the starting point for anyone is the decision to develop this trait.

It will not be an easy process, and if you stumble along the way that doesn't mean all is lost. Far from it. Maybe you will have your own moment face down in the stream of life, but with a helping hand you will get back on your feet and march on.

One of my great friends from the United States Marine Corps is retired Sergeant Major Michael Mack, a drill instructor who grew up in humble surroundings in New Jersey. He is the embodiment of self-discipline, and that value enabled him to rise through the ranks. It also helped get him back on his feet – literally – when his Marine Corps career almost came to an abrupt end after just one year, when his vehicle rolled down a mountainside, leaving him badly injured. This is Mike's inspirational story, combining one value we have already looked at, overcoming obstacles, and the focus of this chapter, self-discipline:

Discipline is doing those challenging things that we may not want to do or it may hurt to do but that need to be done. It is a standard of 100 per cent, whether that is getting dressed quickly when you are going through Marine Corps recruit training or being on time every time, making sure you have the necessary level of fitness, being prepared to do something over and over again to make it right. This is all self-discipline, and it pays off. Without it, you can't go into combat, and equally in civilian life it's just as important. It's a value that I have passed on to my children and I'm grateful to see how they have achieved in their lives because of it.

In the Marines, we believe that drill is inherently linked to discipline. You have to march straight up and down, your arms have to go a certain distance forward and back, you have to hold your rifle in a precise manner and when you stand at the position of attention you don't move at all or the instructor will end up in your face with the hairdryer treatment. The instructor can look straight at 112 men standing at attention and see with periphery vision if someone is moving. Maintaining that position wasn't easy when a mosquito landed on my neck during boot camp at Parris Island, South Carolina. The blood was running down my neck but I was determined not to move and there wasn't any sympathy coming my way from the drill instructor, who simply said, 'Let him eat, Mack. They gotta eat too.' I never scratched it. Now *that's* self-discipline.

The thing about the Marines is that the values are indoctrinated into you; it's done in a relatively short space of time but you carry them throughout your whole life. It was this self-discipline that kept my life on the path I wanted when it seemed that my career might be over.

I was doing well in the Marines when everything changed in an instant. A car was coming the other way in the wrong lane and to avoid it I ended up rolling down a mountain and breaking my neck. My car was totally destroyed but somehow I walked a mile and a half back to the road. I was fortunate that two of my buddies had been on the same trip in a different car and they came along and I told them to take me back to the barracks. Instead, I woke up in the hospital after passing out in their car. Five different medical professionals were around me and I was eventually told that I had a fracture of my spine and they didn't know if I would be able to walk again, never mind be a Marine. I was flown to San Diego California military medical facility where I was put in a Minerva brace, which meant for ten months I couldn't shower or bath properly.

I have to admit I had some negative thoughts. The Marines had been my way out and there was a real possibility I wouldn't be a Marine anymore. But I wasn't giving up. A physio was assigned to me and I did exactly what I had to and every day I asked the physio if I was still going to be a Marine. At the start she said, 'No way', but as time went on and I got stronger I convinced her and the Marines to let me do a medical evaluation. After thirteen months I was doing the same fitness test that every Marine had to go through: 100 sit-ups in two minutes, twenty dead-hang pull-ups and a three-mile run inside twenty-five minutes. I made it; I was still a Marine. I shed tears of joy. I served my country and have many great memories, and that self-discipline is with me to this day and will never leave me.

Mike's story is an extreme example of self-discipline. But it goes to show that if you build self-discipline into your life, every day, then when you need it most, it is there to draw upon. Rather than waiting until you really need it, start building self-discipline into your life today, so that you have it as a weapon in your arsenal when times get tough.

Making a contract with yourself

First, we have to address how to identify and frame your long-term goal. What is it that gets you out of bed? What do you want and why do you want it? And when setting your goal, don't hold back. Be honest about what you want, no matter how unachievable it may seem at the time. So, how do we identify those goals? I've found that aligning your goals with your larger purpose is important. This helps you to combine WHAT you want to achieve with WHY you want to achieve it. This will help you with motivation and the self-discipline to keep moving forwards, especially when things get tough.

Throughout my life, I have always set out what I want to do and why, and the WHY aspect is so important. It's different for everyone, but it is crucial that you take the time to understand what motivates and drives you. My WHY is about life fulfilment and to inspire people and teams to achieve their impossible dreams. I get an incredible amount of personal reward from both of these drivers. I urge you to look deep inside yourself, so that you can find your WHY. It might be something you want to achieve for yourself, or for someone you care for. Mike, who we met in the first section, decided on his WHY when he was just seven years old:

There was a time when, as a child, I came home from school and all the lights in the house were out. I didn't know why. I rang my mum and she just told me to go and do my homework and then I was sent to stay overnight with my aunt and uncle because the reason there was no light, or heating for that matter, was because my mum couldn't afford the electricity. One night I went to say goodnight before I left for my uncle's house and heard my mum cry. I vowed then as a seven-year-old that I would make sure that my mother would never want for anything ever again. I excelled in school and sport and was offered scholarships, but they weren't full scholarships so I couldn't afford to go to university. The Marines was my way to fulfil that commitment.

Once you have identified your WHY, you have taken the first step on the path to achieving WHAT you want to do. The next step in committing to achieving your goals is to write them down. Develop an action plan that clearly outlines your goals and how you intend to achieve them. Break them down into smaller steps, which are process goals that lead you toward your longer-term goal.

This is where the self-discipline comes in. To achieve these process goals you have set yourself requires a self-discipline that is relentless and ruthless, putting aside how you feel in the moment and concentrating on your long-term goal instead of any short-term desires. So, when you don't want to go to the gym, you do; when you don't want to go for the evening walk, you do; when you wake up longing up for another hour in bed, you get up and go – always with an eye to that ultimate goal.

Setting goals is crucial throughout life – whatever stage or age you're at. Goals can give your life meaning and provide you with a clear sense of direction that drives you forwards. The next step to ensuring you reach those goals is making a contract with yourself, recognising and formalising the self-discipline you will need in order to achieve, and holding yourself accountable for it.

Marines have an unwritten and unbreakable contract with

each other: we are a team and we will not let each other down. You need to make a contract like this with yourself – one where you will not let *yourself* down. Define the terms of your contract: what standards will you hold yourself to in order to achieve your goal? And how will you enforce them? So, find your WHY, create your values and make a contract with yourself to stick to them. Set your goals and build an action plan with clear steps, monitoring your pathway as you go. Always reassess your progress regularly, as you may want to re-set and establish new goals. Ask yourself every single day: 'Did I hit my target?', 'Am I moving forwards?', 'What do I need to do next?', 'How can I improve?' This is how people and teams raise the bar, and with the same process you can do it too in your life.

All of this will lead to building a mindset that has self-discipline at its core. When you set out on this contract with yourself, you may lack this self-discipline. That's fine. There's no point beating yourself up about it, because you've already taken the first step. It does take time but achieving those small process goals will organically lead to an increase in self-discipline. You will start to see your thinking shift, even when the pressure is on to cave in to outside pressures or temptation. A self-disciplined mind is able to think critically, demonstrating logic and reason in the face of emotional turmoil. So be patient and allow the self-discipline to grow. Do this and you'll be on your way to achieving things you never thought possible. This method always worked for me, and it will for you too.

The power of persistence

In the Royal Marines, we regard ourselves as world-class, and I see no reason why every person shouldn't aim for that standard in whatever they do – to be the best barber on the high street; to be as good a classroom assistant as you can possibly be; to reach the highest possible standard as a worker in whatever business or industry you are in. There is no special quality that means some people can achieve this while others cannot. It is simply a matter of constantly and persistently practising self-discipline until it becomes second nature.

It's important to understand, however, that change and achievement don't just happen because you dream about them. That's just the starting point. To realise your goals, you have to make good choices, apply yourself and work hard. Failures are inevitable, especially if your goal is high. Rather than be disheartened by failure, use it and learn from it. Keep trying, over and over again. It's amazing what can be achieved with a dream, dogged determination and hard work.

I have seen this unfold before my own eyes, and one great example of it in action is that of a woman, Jane, who was on a one-year course with me, studying rehabilitation along with many other servicemen and women across different Armed Forces. I was a physical training instructor and it seemed a natural move to sub-specialise into rehabilitation so that I could help others in need; something that I got great fulfilment from.

Jane's story is, for me, one of self-discipline personified. It was clear from early on in the course that she had hit a bit of a brick wall. Her knowledge of anatomy and physiology was below par and for the first three months of the course, she seemed lost and was pulling her hair out. The majority of those around her were going along quite comfortably, whereas she would be up all hours trying to make sense of the course. This part of the course was not coming naturally to her – as can be the case with all of us when put in a certain context – but what Jane did was to engage her self-discipline, pushing to identify *what* she was struggling with and then working her way through it. This allowed her to chip away at the wall she had, metaphorically, hit.

I watched her perseverance pay off and by the sixth month she had not only grasped a full understanding of that part of the course, but had overtaken some of the others who had appeared to be more naturally gifted. By the end of the course, she was up in the top third. That self-discipline gave her a relentless attitude to succeed and it was a joy to watch someone dig so deep and truly believe they could accomplish their goals and then see it blossom into success at the end. It would have been easy for Jane to throw in the towel and walk away, to simply accept that the course was not for her and go back to the role she had. Nobody would have thought less of her, but Jane simply didn't accept that this challenge could not be surmounted by a self-disciplined pursuit of her goal. She had a lot of help along the way, but she was also prepared to push through the discomfort, frustration and even maybe a little embarrassment to make the grade. What I learned from this experience is that it's not about talent – it's about attitude!

It is something that we see all the time in Marines training. I remember when I first joined up, one of my fellow trainees was this expert in karate, and for the first few days he was showing off his black belt moves. It was very impressive, and I could see the instructors loved him at the start. I looked at him and thought, *Oh no, if this is the standard I'm up against, I've got no chance* . . . But then things changed.

He was a guy of about twenty-five who enjoyed standing out from the crowd, being the one in the spotlight, but he could not get his head around the discipline required. He only lasted three weeks. He may have been an extremely talented karate expert, but he was not going to be a Marine. The Marines aren't looking for the fastest, the fittest, or the black belts. They are looking for people who never give in, who are team players and selfless. He wasn't a team player; he was all about himself, and it was clear that he wasn't going to last the course. While this lad had certain flashy skills, he didn't have the persistence needed to grow day-in day-out. He was all surface and lacked substance, and he was without the humility needed to recognise that and change.

He fell further behind, until he was ending up at the back of every activity; his confidence was shattered. Ultimate success and fulfilment were going to be found in the self-discipline required to work hard on every detail, but he couldn't handle that. This is a familiar tale – those who will chip and chip away doing the right thing will get there in the end, while the shooting stars can often crash to earth when the going gets tough. As I say, it's the difference between ability and attitude.

Building a routine

Developing self-discipline is a process, and routines are critical to this. If you have one that isn't effective then you are building in a mechanism that reinforces bad practices. Being lazy and ill-disciplined in one area of life will lead to sloppiness in other areas. So, if instead of getting up and seeking to achieve your goals, you choose to stay in bed or spend hours on the PlayStation, this will have a knock-on impact, not least on your mental health. Each time you *don't* pursue the path of self-discipline, it makes it that bit harder to be proactive the next time you're faced with a choice. It's not all bad news however, because conversely, each time you execute a bit of self-discipline, it will make it easier the next time. In this way an effective routine will pave the way to a self-disciplined way of thinking and acting that leads to sustained success. 'Sound in body and sound in mind' is the Royal Marines physical training motto for a reason.

Take, for example, diet and fitness. During training, the Marines make it abundantly clear that both are paramount. You don't see too many tubby Marines, and if you do see some veterans with a spare tyre, believe me – it does not go down too well, because the values that are ingrained into you really do become part of a way of life, and that goes for whether you're in the Corps or have long since moved on to civilian life.

Frankly speaking, diet and nutrition is an area where it is clear the UK desperately needs to improve, because statistics show that the level of obesity is rising rapidly and is out of control. I know there can be various reasons for those who struggle with weight gain, but I really believe that the disciplined model of the Marines offers hope.

The old saying goes that you are what you eat, and I would recommend a simple, self-disciplined plan that focuses on 'what goes in must equal calories burned', and that way you will keep your weight under control. Simply put, if you put too much in and don't exercise, then you get fat, and if you don't put enough into the body and over-exercise, then the body can break down. This simplified yet balanced way of controlling diet is key, and when you start eating the right foods, fresh fruit and veg, and combine that with good exercise, then you will see improved health benefits. But the key element here is that this can't just be for a few weeks or even months; it has to be a self-disciplined lifestyle change for good.

Self-discipline is not just about denial; it is far more about building in positive habits. The training endured by the Marines means that calorie intake and nutrition must be spot on, so it is emphasised that you never miss a meal. Breakfast, lunch and dinner are all essential, with some additional snacks in between. Proper hydration is also crucial. Lots of protein from fish and meat is important, along with the right portion sizes. If the self-discipline drops, it is picked up on during training, and over the thirty-two weeks there are plenty of moments when an officer will challenge a recruit on why he has failed at a certain task. Missed meals, inadequate sleep or a poorly planned routine are often some of the factors that relate to sub-optimal performance.

Temptation to let self-discipline slip is around all of us, and we can all take a good hard look at ourselves and recognise where it comes from. For modern recruits, one of the most common temptations that they succumb to can be – as I have seen – spending more time on FaceTime or social media than they should, often late into the night, which means they arrive the next day far from being ready to give their best. Social media and that temptation to swipe away the hours can easily eat away at that good routine you're trying to establish in your life. It's the same with those funny YouTube videos. Time is precious, and how we use it reflects our level of self-discipline. This is where building an effective routine that promotes self-discipline will help you to focus on what you *need* to do as opposed to what you *want* to do. So if you know that you have a particular area of weakness, build it into your routine and put boundaries around it: restrict yourself to half an hour of Twitter, allow yourself chocolate once a week. And every time you're tempted to push that boundary, remind yourself that doing so will only make it harder the next time.

The temptation to put things off until tomorrow rarely leads to good results. Instead, you create poor routines that are often characterised by your inability to resist temptation. So build yourself a good routine, and every time you stick to it, remember that you're making it that bit easier for your future self.

Setting boundaries

As human beings we have conflicting thoughts. On the one hand, we all seem to have a naturally rebellious side, and yet at the same time we have a real need for discipline and rules in the way in which we engage with others in life. This can be confusing and contradictory at times, but such boundaries are critical in life. We all need them, and without them we are lost. Boundaries at home, in the classroom or in the workplace help us understand what is acceptable and what is not. We also need enough space and the opportunity to grow within those boundaries, to express ourselves and to leave our own mark on the world.

To me, living life is like being at the firing range, practising with live rounds. You are given the left and right parameters out of which you cannot stray; you must stay within those boundaries or someone will die in real conflict. The instructor will give an order to the recruits – something like: 'Enemy at base of bush, rapid ... FIRE!!' – and you open up with a hail of bullets, but this must be done in a very disciplined and well-practised manner within the constraints of those boundaries. This is non-negotiable – lives are on the line, after all – otherwise in combat you will not just be a threat to your enemy but also a danger to your brothers by your side.

We understand that the boundaries are there to give us structure and direction, but they must also allow us the freedom to operate within them. This is key to being self-disciplined in your own life. When you have clear and well-thought-out objectives, you can be decisive with a degree of confidence that you are operating within the boundaries of what is acceptable.

This might sound contradictory, but operating within boundaries actually brings a certain freedom with it. Once you know that you cannot set foot beyond a certain boundary, you no longer have to grapple with the decision of how far to go. For this reason it is crucial not to shift those boundaries. Work out what is an acceptable and realistic boundary line for you and never go beyond it. This removes any element of negotiation with yourself and strengthens that self-discipline.

Inspiration as a tool – from within yourself, and from others

A self-disciplined mind that enhances your self-belief is absolutely crucial but, equally, sometimes it is the example of others that takes you to another level. For my good friend Dr Lara Herbert, a former Royal Navy Commando, the understanding of self-discipline came early in life when she lived in her native Zimbabwe, before coming to England and having that value emboldened by the Marines. As Lara explains:

> There's no doubt that the forces helped me to hone my innate self-discipline, which I believe I learned at boarding school in Zimbabwe. My parents lived several hours away from the nearest schools, so day school wasn't an option! Students in Zimbabwe have a real hunger to learn. They know that good grades at school open doors to exciting career opportunities, often abroad. I went to a wonderful, multi-racial school in Harare. Coming from a white, privileged background, I had an overwhelming assumption that if I just cruised along at school, I would do just fine in life. Working alongside my black friends, however, gave me the kick I needed. I saw the hours they put in to studying for their O-level examinations, many rising before 4 a.m.

daily to study. I also saw the outstanding results they were achieving. It struck me then that if I really wanted to achieve my life goals, I was going to have to up my game. Many of these friends are now leading experts in their chosen fields, some working at a global level. Their self-discipline paid off.

These young women were not Marines, but they had the same mentality that was drummed in me on the Commando course that there is no limit to what you can achieve. Individuals who embrace the idea of self-discipline are far more likely to do better than those who build barriers for themselves.

Lara proved her own levels of self-discipline by becoming only the second woman in history to complete the Commando course and has gone on to have a very successful medical career. Having earned her green beret, she was then deployed to Afghanistan, and I can honestly say that I never considered her gender; to me, Lara was simply a sister who bled green just like all my brothers – and sometimes in training she left the lads in her wake.

So, self-discipline is not just about you; it is also about the effect that it has on others around you. Self-discipline can inspire others to be more self-disciplined themselves; they might look at you and decide that the commitment you are showing is something that is missing in their lives. Throughout Marines training, self-discipline is always understood within the context that we are working within a team. It is a collective effort, and therefore all within the troop are accountable to each other because we regard ourselves as a family unit. This same principle can be followed in every family, every school class, every office, because that sense of accountability will act as a force-multiplier to drive the collective self-discipline aimed towards a common goal.

When someone fails to stick to the standards required, it's not only the recruit who is questioned, but also the Marines around him. So, if an individual's kit isn't ready for inspection because they have wasted too much time on their phone, the instructor will ask the others why they didn't address it with him. The self-discipline of the Marines extends to taking ownership of the performances of others as well as your own. This is something I have seen with my children when, for example, my youngest daughter Casey passed on her dedicated experience of preparing for school exams to her younger brother Charlie. Her voice was heard, probably more easily than mine or my wife Suzanne's, and in a very practical way she was looking out for her brother, to make sure he understood the most productive, self-disciplined way to revise. Ultimately, of course, while he could learn from his sister's example and experience Charlie was responsible for his own self-discipline, and had to hold himself accountable.

So, embark on a journey where you become accountable to yourself and take ownership of your actions. This will have even more impact in a team environment, when you make a pledge to your team to live out your values, where you commit to owning each other's destinies and where you mutually agree to go that extra mile for the team. In effect, you hold both the success and failure of others in your hands.

In time, your self-disciplined approach will begin to reap rewards as you form new habits that will enhance your overall performance. Self-discipline is a value that can *always* be found in people who achieve. They are driven, focused and possess a can-do attitude that simply gets things done. Take control of your own actions, build that routine, set those boundaries, and whatever you do, stick at it.

When life comes at us like a hailstorm of bullets, that's when we need to possess the self-discipline to rise to the challenge, to embrace the conflict and pain, and keep a cold-eyed focus on our goals.

CHAPTER 3: SELF-DISCIPLINE LESSON SUMMARY

Remember . . .

- Make a contract with yourself based on your values and find your WHY.
- Build a routine with self-discipline at its core.
- Self-discipline will take you to levels and places you never thought possible.

Step 1 – WHAT is self-discipline?

Self-discipline is about making a conscious decision to get up and act. It's about building positive behaviours that allow you to maintain a high level of focus on your goals. It will enable you to remain in control of yourself and it will drive the way you act in any given situation, from getting out of bed to complex work activities. Self-discipline can be learned and developed; the more you train it, the more successful you become.

Step 2 – WHY is self-discipline important?

When you consistently practice self-discipline you will notice that it gives you the power and inner strength to overcome challenges such as addictions, procrastination and laziness. In time it will build a habit of behaviour where you always follow through and Never Give In, allowing you to achieve things you never thought possible.

Step 3 – HOW to become self-disciplined in your life.

- Self-discipline starts from the moment you wake up.
- Make an unbreakable contract with yourself; be accountable to others but mainly to yourself.
- Start small, find an achievable goal, make a plan and write it down, be self-disciplined enough to see it through to the end.
- Set non-negotiable boundaries for yourself.
- Incorporate this behaviour into your routine, make it the new you, and admire how much you have changed.

CHAPTER 4

Determination

Definition: A quality that drives you to do
or achieve something that is difficult.

No limits

The massive amount of blood flowing from his groin meant
my great mate and former Royal Marines Colour Sergeant
Lee Spencer had just fifteen minutes to live. Lying on the
motorway hard shoulder in the dark, one leg severed from
his body and the other twisted in the wrong direction, the
odds of survival were not exactly in his favour.

Lee had enjoyed a great career as a Marine, serving with
distinction in Afghanistan among other places, but his world
was turned upside down when travelling home one night on
the motorway. His car suffered a puncture, which led him

to post on social media: 'Can this journey get any worse?' Sadly, for him, it did. Further down the motorway, a car had broken down and he stopped to help. Four guys and a heavily pregnant woman had been in the car and he managed to get them to a safe place on the roadside. As he was checking them over, another car hit their stationary vehicle. The engine block shot out and crashed straight into Lee, taking off one leg straight away and sending him 15 metres up in the air and down a bank.

He quickly realised that those who he had just saved were not coming to help him. They had left him for dead. As a result of his Marines training, he recognised that he was bleeding out and in shock, and at one point felt he had to make THE call to say a final goodbye to his wife and family. In that moment, however, he refused to give in and instead summoned the determination to stay alive. He decided to take ownership of what appeared to be an impossible situation with no way out.

Pushing himself beyond his limits, he crawled under the metal barrier and onto the hard shoulder. This was when he first noticed that his leg had gone. At that moment, a noble passer-by noticed the accident and stopped. The man tried to apply a tourniquet, but that wasn't working. Seeing the man's daughter with him, Lee, barely conscious at this point, told him to stop the bleeding by getting his daughter to stand on the artery at his groin area. That stopped the bleeding and kept him alive just long enough for the paramedics to arrive. That man and his daughter saved my brother's life.

Lee refused to allow the situation to overtake him and when he woke up the next day and realised that he had gone from a highly capable Royal Marine to someone with life-changing disabilities, Lee made a pact with himself that he was not going to be defined by his disability. When I think of determination and what it means, I see my friend of twenty-five years, Lee Spencer, as the embodiment of that value. This is how he describes it:

> The night before I had looked in the mirror and I knew who I was: I was a Marine who was operating behind enemy lines. All my life I had wanted to be a Marine. The next day I woke up a disabled person. I had to redefine myself, but I also decided that I was going to be the best disabled person I could be. I fought to stay alive; I was on the edge. Medically I had lost half my body's blood, and when people approach that mark, they die. So, when I woke up, my first thought was, *I'm here. I've lost my leg but I'm still here.*

Circumstances, people around you and even society can make you believe that there is no point going on, that you will not be able to find a way forward. Lee Spencer could have given up, but that wasn't his way. Instead, he would prove to the world that there were no limits on what he could do if he applied determination to the situation. And that's a value for everyone, in every situation – you can reach for that dream job, you can overcome that setback, you can defy every obstacle in your way and continue to fight on. You can find that determination. As the Marines teach: 'It's a state of mind: no limits.'

Of course, in life, circumstances will come along that

drain the determination from our hearts and minds. Often, fear is involved. But determination can overcome fear. And determination can grow from the smallest seed. Lee told me about the transformation that took place in his life, from being a scared little boy to a Marine who pushed back on the brink of death:

> My trauma came as a boy, at seven years of age. My father was a violent alcoholic who used to beat up my mum. She used to cry out for me to come and help and I would stand at the door and freeze through fear. I always wanted to be a Marine. I wanted to be brave, to have courage. I always had a deep insecurity about my own bravery.
>
> Everything in life I was useless at; I had failed at so much. I was terrible at sport and when I first showed an interest in joining the Marines I was told by the recruiting officer, 'I don't think you are what we are looking for.'
>
> That all changed when, during my training, I was doing an exercise called Running Man.
>
> Over and over, we were asked to do a navigation exercise, and after the first and second long-distance route marches, I sat down, exhausted. 'I can't do another one, I really can't,' I said, but then I kept going and it shocked me. I *felt* exhausted, I *believed* I was exhausted, and yet I was able to keep going. I realised right there and then that I didn't know my limits, and I believe that every human being can reach those same depths of determination.

You have to dig deep. But no matter how scared or small you feel, we all have within us that seed of determination, and if you keep feeding it, it can grow into something life-changing – or, in Lee's case, life-saving.

Shared determination

The secret to feeding that seed of determination lies in action. Lee's determination didn't take long to translate into action. The accident that ripped away his leg and Marine career happened on 5 January 2014, and by December 2015 he was rowing the Atlantic with three other amputees. Not only did they succeed, but these four wounded servicemen set a new world record time. Not satisfied with that, he raced Superman Henry Cavill up the Gibraltar Rock, and then decided to row the Atlantic in an attempt to beat the able-bodied, single-handed and unsupported world record.

To help raise money for the transatlantic challenge, Lee also set up a charity boxing match which saw him the share the ring with former world super-middleweight champion Glenn Catley for three painful rounds. I was ringside with him, and despite getting put down on the canvas twice, Lee kept getting back up and, as you can imagine, received a standing ovation for his efforts. When the time came for Lee to start his mammoth task, back home I set up our own 'Row with Lee' charity campaign. It really caught on and we had people up and down the country joining in as we tracked him across the Atlantic on his two-month voyage. Even the Marine recruits and staff at Lympstone stopped their training to 'row with Lee', taking turns on the rowing machines to cover the full 3,500 miles between us.

It all seemed to be going to plan until I got an unexpected phone call from Lee stuck somewhere in the middle of the Atlantic. I was thrilled to hear from him, but then the mood changed as it quickly became clear that Lee was struggling and was going to need every ounce of his determination to carry on. As Lee himself put it: 'I was in the depths of despair. I was mentally and physically exhausted.'

Lee admitted that he felt both scared and alone, in the middle of the Atlantic Ocean, with the nearest person to him at that exact moment somewhere on the International Space Station. Feeling totally isolated, he was calling me up as his mate to give him some friendly support and to remind him WHY he was doing it. I felt so honoured that he rang me, and it gave me the chance to tell him about all those wonderful people around the country he had inspired and who were 'rowing with Lee', from infant school children to eighty-year-olds. It was very emotional; he was crying and so was I. Out of that conversation, however, he found the strength to drive forward from his lowest ebb. The power of friendship can spark that determination to keep going, to find a way forward. So if you find yourself fighting to keep going, when you feel the world has left you battered and bruised, reach out. It is amazing how much it can strengthen your resolve when you share your feelings with someone who actually cares.

I'm very thankful for the friendship that I have with Lee, and I was so pleased to be able to give something back, to help my friend on that day. All I had done was remind him that he wasn't alone and that he had no limits. It was something that he already knew; he just needed to hear it from someone else. Determination doesn't mean doing something entirely on your own – it can also mean knowing when to reach out to a sympathetic ear for that extra boost. Lee and I have learnt a lot about the strength of our combined determination through our deep friendship, especially during those times when things got tough and the outcome was uncertain. We have known and worked together for over twenty-five years, and have developed a relationship that is much like being brothers. With that comes a sense of admiration and genuine love for him and his family that has been borne from sharing incredible moments that have shaped our lives. These include the Wounded Warrior Games in USA, freefall parachuting, theatre entry operations in Iraq, the Marines display team, our world records, and then, as Lee's commanding officer, supporting him and his family when he got injured. During that time, we have developed an understanding that translates into an unwritten pledge and a determination to be there for each other, no matter what. And we both thrive on each other's achievements, especially when we are being pushed to the limits of what is humanly possible.

As Marines, we expect struggles, but we do also acknowledge that it is these moments that bring us even closer together. Again, there is strength in shared determination. When a friend feels they are finished, you can take the next step for them. The collective will of a band of brothers and sisters, which is how we regard ourselves in the Armed Forces, can be so powerful when engendered throughout communities. It's pride in the collective effort which we see in great charitable endeavours. That same determined shared togetherness and sense of belonging can change people and teams for the better.

Lee not only found the will to keep going, but he broke the able-bodied, solo unsupported transatlantic world record, which was ninety-six days. He did it in an incredible sixty days, beating the existing record by more than a month. He now holds a total of four world records, and more challenges lie ahead. He is one of my real-life heroes who I'm proud to call a brother.

Finding a new 100 per cent

What Lee had understood about determination is that you always have more to give. And that when you fail at something, that is exactly the moment when you find out how much more you have in you – when determined resilience comes into play. As he puts it:

When you think you have given everything, you are only halfway there. I now give talks for a living and the focus is on failure. The biggest highlight of my career came when a youth club in Plymouth redecorated the outside of their club and after one of my talks they put across the wall something I said to them: 'Dare to dream – and if you don't fail, you're not dreaming big enough.'

So much of this world, especially on social media, portrays a lie of how well people are living. They pose in a certain way and look a certain way; they'll not describe how awful their life is because they feel they have to keep up a pretence of how great life is, and in the long run that is only damaging to themselves. But life is not always easy,

and to get through tough times you need that determination alongside humility — being honest with yourself. If the
attitude is, 'That obstacle in front of me was put there by
society and it's not my fault that I can't get over it', then
you won't. But, if you face the truth that you failed because
you were not strong enough, or you were not fast enough,
then you go away and work on those things. Then you go
again and again if needed, because failure is not final when
you have the Marine value of determination.

You see, there is a false expectation from most people that
we must succeed at everything we do straight away. Maybe
you are someone who feels this way, but let me tell you, that
is not the reality. You need to shift your thinking. As flawed
human beings, we fail all the time, and I would argue that if
your life is free of failure then you have not pushed yourself
hard enough. You must learn to accept defeat before you can
discover how to succeed, and so failure should be seen as a
natural and acceptable part of the process of learning to be
become successful. Some people are afraid to fail or to take a
chance for fear of looking silly, but this type of thinking both
restricts us and deprives us of the benefits we could gain from
being brave enough to try new experiences just beyond our
comfort zone, to really embrace the possibility of failure and
grow through it. When we take those chances in life, even if
things don't go as we hoped or if the outcome is not what we
wished for, there is so much growth that takes place in those
low moments. The best of life begins with a challenge, and
no matter what you've gone through, get back off the floor,
learn from it, never give in and keep chasing your dreams.

As one of the officers commanding Royal Marines training, I witnessed the value of determination in the face of
failure in one particular recruit who stands out from the
thousands that I have worked with over the years. At the
Commando training base in Lympstone, the last six weeks
are critical, when we put the recruits through the final phase
of training that culminates in the world-famous Commando
tests. Up to this point, they have been tested in the various
attributes required, but the Commando phase examines all
these skills in tandem to confirm their suitability to earn and
wear the coveted green beret. There are four Commando
tests based around physical fitness and mental fortitude: the
endurance course, including two and a half miles of underwater tunnels and obstacles; the nine-mile speed march as
part of a squad, carrying all your kit with everyone finishing
together in ninety minutes; the assault courses, a normal
one plus the Tarzan course, which is suspended 30 feet in
trees above the ground; and finally the 30-mile route march
across the expanse of Dartmoor. These take place on four
consecutive days, when you are totally fatigued at the end
of thirty-two punishing weeks of training, so we really do
push people beyond what they believe to be their limit. As
I like to say, 'Tell me you can't do it and I'll show you how
you can.' You find out the depth of your determination and
then the Marines show you how to dig that little bit deeper,
to take just one more step forward . . .

Being determined to give 100 per cent is commendable,
but I am a firm believer that as we go through life we can
continually push what that 100 per cent looks like. Of course,
you can't give more than 100 per cent – but you can shift

where you draw that line. One more step, one more shove, one more hour of revision for that exam, one more hour of training a week to achieve that goal, and your new 100 per cent has grown just a little bit more that day.

When it came to the final test – the route march of 30 miles – this particular young recruit got to the 28-mile point and signalled that he simply could not go on. His green beret was just 2 miles in front of him, but he wasn't going to make it. He was in agony. And in the Marines there are no exceptions; the standards are not up for discussion. He pulled out, and he did not get his green beret. It didn't matter that he had progressed very well throughout his training up to this moment; he had fallen short on the final examination.

On medical inspection after he dropped out, it became clear why he couldn't complete the march. From early on in the fourth test he was aware that he had injured his ankle and it had been bothering him throughout. It turned out it wasn't just a sore ankle. He had actually snapped it completely 2 miles into the march, and then continued another 26 miles with a broken ankle! Taking that into consideration, it could easily have been argued that the young man had demonstrated such fortitude that he deserved his green beret. From my recollection, nobody had previously gone 26 miles with a broken ankle of that severity, and that level of determination was exactly what we were looking for in a Royal Marine Commando. But the standards of the Royal Marines are unwavering, they are set in stone, irrelevant of personal circumstances or favour, and we had to tell that young recruit that he had failed to achieve his green beret.

You can imagine the recruit's overwhelming sense of

devastation, and if he had decided to walk away from the Marines, I couldn't have blamed him. But his resources of determination had not been sucked dry. Instead, he once again showed he belonged in the green beret brotherhood. He had already gained the respect of both his comrades and the instructors after we all witnessed his tenacity on Dartmoor, but now he was determined to complete his mission. After almost a year of rehabilitation, he went back for those crucial final six weeks of training and this time he made it. I can honestly say it was a very special moment to be there when he received his green beret. That is the depth of determination you need in life and you can have that when you keep demanding more from yourself.

The importance of adversity

Of course, determination goes hand in hand with adversity – as we saw in Lee's story, and that of the young recruit with the broken ankle. It is through pushing ourselves through adversity that we become stronger.

Some obstacles seem immovable, yet the toughest, most challenging hurdles that we face come from within. Life always presents us with problems of varying degrees of difficulty. It's not so much what happens to us that actually makes a difference, but what we do next in the face of these life challenges, particularly those that feel insurmountable, that will determine the final outcome. Such obstacles are extremely difficult to overcome because in many instances we are often blinded to their existence. Once you identify these obstacles and endeavour to understand how they affect you, you must then learn to deal with them in a practical and effective way by coming up with a plan that will help you to move in the right direction once more. The determination is to then see the plan through to its conclusion, no matter what. But that will require you to show new levels of commitment, self-discipline and a mindset totally embodied by determination.

We learn this principle in the Marines when placed in extreme conditions such as the Arctic wastes of northern Norway, where I have operated many times in sub-zero temperatures and where training scenarios quickly turn into real-life survival situations. The coldest I ever experienced was a combined wind chill of -76 degrees Celsius. You spit and it's ice before it hits the ground, your eyes stick together because the moisture in your eyes freezes, and your skin literally freezes straight away. If you don't cover up your skin, then it turns black and dies.

Why is the training so hard? We talk about 'train hard; fight easy', which in practice means we always train to just beyond our limits, so that when it comes to the crunch (as life usually does), you've been there before in training, and you know you can do it. It's about developing the belief that you have that inner resolve and determination to continue no matter what the circumstances are. It's how we become accustomed to uncertainty and learn to expect the unexpected. It's yet another example of that Marine state of mind where you simply refuse to give in.

After Marines training, you swiftly realise that there are certain times when you are expected to perform physical feats of endurance that far outweigh anything you did in basic training. Every two-year cycle we were deployed by land or by sea to some far-flung place where we would be required to live in the field for days or weeks at a time. Whether in the jungles of Brunei, the great deserts of the Middle East or the Scottish Highland mountains, it always involved carry-ing – and sometimes skiing with – huge backpacks over vast distances, in all kinds of weather conditions, in some of the world's harshest types of terrain.

We used to live in something called 'tent sheets' in north-ern Norway, inside the Arctic Circle, which were heavy-duty diamond-shaped pieces of fabric that we buttoned together to make one big tent. We often lived high above the treeline, and the ice froze our tent sheets together and one person then had to carry them all. It took a few of you to roll it up and place it on top of one of our large packs. This added a further back-breaking 120lbs to your kit.

I recall carrying a frozen seven-man tent up one of Norway's highest mountains, and it remains one of the hard-est single feats of physical endurance that I ever accomplished. It wasn't just the weight, or the height of the mountain, but the fact that you had to reverse ski up the mountain in a technique known as 'Herringboning'. You point uphill and splay the ski tips out before taking each step uphill. It is ball-breaking work, especially when cold, wet, tired and hungry with more than 200lbs on your back (I weighed 180lbs), and it took every ounce of my being to continue to put one ski in front of the other and just keep going.

It takes an incredible amount of determination to push yourself to the limit of human endurance day after day. This goes beyond the physical limits and into the realms of mental fortitude. But you learn a lot about yourself at times like this and a great deal of personal growth takes place in these moments. And when you come through the other side of the pain, when you make a stand with yourself to never give in, to never ever give up, then that feeling of pride and strength is unbelievable. You feel invincible, as if nothing will ever stop you ever again.

The importance of routine

We talked in the previous chapter about the importance of routine in building self-discipline. The same applies to determination. When you have proven to yourself just how determined you can be, despite an almighty setback, it is a strength that never leaves you; it remains an indelible part of your character. But unless it is practised, over and over again, it can diminish. Over the years I can think of many times when it would have been easy to give up, but, as Aristotle said, 'You are what you continuously do.' So, if you give up once, it becomes easier to give up again, and soon it becomes a habit – one that is hard to break. But the counterbalance to this is that having pushed through adversity once, it can also become a habit! It is hard to take one more step forward, it is hard to get back up off the floor after being knocked down, and it is even harder to find the resolve to persevere when you feel that you cannot give any more and that all is lost. But once 'never giving up' becomes a habit, and once you have made a pact with yourself to never quit, then that is when you can start to achieve your 'impossible' dreams.

I don't think there is any better example of such character than the great Captain Sir Tom Moore, who sadly passed away in 2020, but who left an incredible legacy. At ninety-nine years of age, he decided to raise money for the NHS by walking around his garden 100 times, despite the fact he was being treated for skin cancer and had broken a hip in 2018.

Captain Tom's determination was an inspiration to everyone in the UK at a time of national crisis. The NHS was creaking under the weight of the pandemic and the thousands being struck down, while the lack of personal protection equipment was causing fear and anxiety. Then along came a proud 99-year-old Second World War army veteran who demonstrated the determination and resilience that was going to be needed in order for the country to get through this crisis. Raising £40 million for the NHS was an incredible feat and I think it's fair to say that his values reached out and touched every area of society. A true hero.

Determination in the detail

The determination of the Marines is drilled into young recruits because we value the life of every Marine and see the importance of training them to a very high standard so that they have the skills, values and self-belief that maximise their performance and enhance operational readiness.

This was brought home to me in a huge way in 2003 when, as one of the senior commanders in Charlie Company 40 Commando, I was whisked away with the rest of the command team to a secret Special Forces location within a giant

US-led desert base in Kuwait called Camp Commando. As 'first on the ground' commanders, we were afforded the privilege of entering the inner sanctum, where we would focus on mission planning. It consisted of a top-secret, secured, multi-layered entry system, at the heart of which was the model briefing room for the invasion of southern Iraq. There were only about a dozen people in this secret theatre entry mission planning room out of the 330,000 Coalition troops that were positioned on the Kuwaiti border waiting to go in – and I was one of them. Our Company commander gave his orders, and we then came up with our troop mission to fit in with his overall plan.

One of the areas that we had to assault was a set of buildings which we believed contained enemy Iraqi forces. We studied the aerial photographs that we had of the buildings so that we could locate the best entry routes while avoiding detection, in order to maintain the element of surprise. I noticed that we didn't have a photograph of one of the building frontages, and this presented an issue. Did it have windows? Did it have a door? Was it a route that we could take to avoid detection? Maybe a sniper would be waiting for us there – which would obviously be disastrous.

This level of detailed planning is critical to mission success; any failure to ensure that we had planned for every possible eventuality would be putting my men at severe risk. I needed to know what was there, so I spoke to a US general and explained the situation. He immediately tasked one of the intelligence analysts to get me the image that I had asked for. Within thirty minutes, the general came back and handed me a 'real-time' satellite photograph of the building. It then dawned on me that they had re-tasked a satellite to get the information that I needed. Re-tasking a satellite is a big deal, and I just thought, *Wow!*

I had witnessed a level of determination that took even me aback. There was a resolve to not unnecessarily put my men's lives at risk by doggedly sourcing the information that was critical to mission success, and there was a willingness on behalf of our allies to support us in any way they could, no matter how difficult the task. It gives an insight into the meticulous nature of operational planning, and I believe offers a reminder to every one of us about our own levels of determination, and the grit and fortitude that are required to get the little details right.

In the same way, I believe that the Royal Marines' value of determination will enable you to thrive when the chips are down, when life seems overwhelming and when the outcome is in doubt. The key is to motivate yourself to take the necessary action that will enable you to overcome the obstacles that stand in your way, to remind yourself that you *can* find a way through it.

Motivation and inspiration can be powerful beasts. If someone has inspired you or made you feel more motivated, then I wholeheartedly recommend getting as close to that person as you can. Study them, engage with them, question them and get into their mindset. Understand their journey and what made them grow into someone who motivates others. Only by understanding them will you be able to comprehend what it is that makes them so special. By all means emulate what you see in these people, but also remember to dig deep inside yourself; work out what makes *you* special and then resolve to grow that.

I've worked alongside people and teams of all ages and genders from across countless industries around the world and watched them as they grow individually and together through hardship, adversity and uncertainty. It has been enlightening for me to observe as they ponder the question of whether they can or can't do something, and then watching how they show new levels grit and determination that they never realised they had in them.

Their 100 per cent had grown, and it is so fulfilling when you play a part in people's growth in this way, where they realise that anything *is* possible and that there are no limits to what can be achieved. It is that epiphany, that moment of unique growth, that defines your determination, and when you realise that, you will never look back. Each time you make the decision to put just one more foot forward, it will make the next time that little bit easier. Determination is a self-sustaining habit!

CHAPTER 4: DETERMINATION LESSON SUMMARY

Remember ...

* Never accept failure – pick yourself back up and keep going. Success will come.
* Be determined to push yourself through adversity so that perseverance and growth become a self-sustaining habit.
* You can grow your 100 per cent every single day by building your levels of resilience and determination.

Step 1 – WHAT is determination?

Determination is the quality that drives you to do or achieve something that is difficult. It is a key value that is linked to how we grow, using our past experiences and the knowledge gained to carry on during tough times when it may seem easier to give up. It manifests as possessing a state of mind where you keep going and Never Give In.

Step 2 – WHY is determination important?

Determination is a particularly important quality because it allows us to keep going, especially in the face of extreme difficulty or where the path forward may not be clear. It affords us the belief and confidence to keep driving towards a goal and gives us the power to surmount the seemingly impossible. Determination allows us to overcome obstacles and march forward towards our desired goals. Ordinary people can achieve extraordinary things by exhibiting determination to overcome hardships and failure, and to drive toward success. DETERMINATION can eventually overcome and dispel FEAR.

Step 3 – HOW to become determined in your life.

* Understand what drives you, motivates you. What is your WHY?
* Define your goals and break each goal into smaller process goals.
* Develop a strategy and attack each smaller goal in turn until it is complete.
* Show determination in the detail; don't let the little things slide, they are important too!
* Understand that there are no limits to what can be achieved when YOU show new levels of commitment, self-discipline and a mindset totally embodied by determination.

CHAPTER 5

Adaptability

Definition: To change your ideas or
behaviours to make them suitable for a
new situation.

Corporal Peter 'Louis' Lewis had 50p in his pocket and one
bag with all his clothes in it. He was fifty years old and a former
Marine who had fallen on hard times. He had also played a key
role in making me the man I am today. Louis, as he is known
to his mates, was and still is my mentor and role model.

It doesn't matter who you are, at any point the tectonic
plates of life can shift you into a tight corner, and that's what
happened with Louis, who had lost his home and so ended
up without a job and living with his brother. It is inevitable
that life will throw a few curveballs your way – what is up to
you is how you adapt to your new circumstances.

Louis may have been out of the Marines for a couple of decades and under the cosh, but his state of mind remained that of a Royal Marine – something that he had forged through his own training in the early 1980s and during subsequent operational tours of duty to the Falklands and Northern Ireland. Suddenly, at fifty years old, finding himself in a new situation looking for civilian employment in an environment where everything felt alien, he had to adapt in a major way to get his life back on track. But the power to adapt is something Louis had learned previously, and he was now able to draw upon those experiences to find a way to change his fortunes. During his time of greatest need, Louis summoned the qualities and values that were central to his DNA and which he had nurtured during his time in the Marines. The training he had received may have taken place thirty years beforehand, but it was about to kick in.

Louis knew he had to put his pride and his preferences to one side while he got himself back on his feet. While his aspirations remained high, he prioritised getting a job – any job – for the immediate future. Within two days he had a job driving a van. Louis didn't want to be a driver, but sometimes you do the things you *need* to do, so that it can set you up to do the things you *want* to. Louis saw the driving job as a necessary stepping-stone, so he knuckled down and got on with it, knowing it would eventually lead to bigger and better things. Louis didn't stop searching and applying, and almost immediately landed a trial shift at a pub.

On his fiftieth birthday Louis was out the door doing his van work at 6 a.m. and then into the kitchen for his three-hour trial, which he passed. This was more like it. Louis grasped the opportunity to work in a pub with both hands and within eight months was a deputy manager. Now he runs a pub for the same company with an annual net turnover of £1.5 million a year.

The adaptability that Louis had learned in his Marines training turned out to be relevant not just for the battlefield but for life in general. And Louis' story is a familiar one. Following the COVID-19 pandemic, millions of people have had to come to terms with new situations and adapt to new challenges. Lives have been turned upside down and some of the stories have been heart-breaking to listen to.

As part of the hospitality industry, Louis was right in the eye of the storm that COVID brought to the economy. He could see the panic in the faces of employees and had to lead them through it. With understanding, kindness and cheerfulness, he led from the front, just as he had always done when leading his Marines, who had included me in Northern Ireland and on subsequent deployments around the world.

Change in our world over the past couple of decades seems to have come at us like a whirlwind. Being accustomed to dealing with the unexpected – and therefore being able to adapt – is now one of the most important skills you can possess. It is also something that is drilled into you as a Marine. The training is purposefully complex in order to stretch your capability to adapt. For example, in an exercise, you might be given instructions to carry out, and then suddenly in the middle of the operation the group might be attacked from behind and casualties will have to be dealt with as you fight off the counter-attack.

In such a circumstance you have to react instantly. Change

has to happen in the moment. You adapt and make changes or you die – it's as simple as that. The same principle can be applied to businesses in the middle of a crisis or a huge change to the way an industry operates. For example, the world of newspapers has had to adapt to the social media age in order to continue to be profitable, while during the pandemic restaurants had to make very quick adjustments to provide their services in new, socially distanced ways. Globally we saw the astonishing adaptability of people fighting to make sure they kept their businesses and jobs alive where possible. Some circumstances are obviously harder to handle than others, and loss in particular tests to the limit that ability to adapt – whether that is a loss of a job, loss of a business, or the loss of a loved one.

It is also important to emphasise that when having to adapt to a situation that has suddenly come about in life, the reaction should not be driven by emotion. I think we can all be guilty of this, and I've frequently seen knee-jerk reactions that have ended in disaster. Instead, taking a tactical knee – pausing to take in all the information required to understand the situation – will always result in a better outcome. Taking a tactical knee allows you to see the bigger picture, to take a more rational approach, to consider hidden pitfalls or opportunities, and to plot a successful route forward. Emotions can also blind us to how the situation may also impact on others, and pausing to put those emotions in context will often prevent a lot of friction and difficulties, whether in a business or social group or family. Practically, this translates into taking some time to accept your initial emotional reaction, pause for thought, and make a considered decision. This can be particularly hard when it is a large or life-changing decision, and the emotions are even more elevated, but this is when it is especially important to take that moment.

So, sometimes we have to adapt fast, and sometimes adapting is a slower process of developing self-awareness and learning to change. In both situations, however, adaptability has the same root, and that is about having a growth mindset.

Embracing change and developing a growth mindset

When I joined the Marines, I had to adapt from being a south London teenager with very few rules and regulations in my life to being in an environment that demanded the highest of standards all the time. It was a complete 180-degree turnaround from where I had come from. Adapting naturally means change, and the majority of us do not like change. Rather, we prefer to find a comfortable place in life and follow that path. But we all now live in a fast-paced, ever-changing world, with few jobs that are guaranteed for a lifetime. Opportunities for change and growth will be presented to you many times and in many guises over the course of your life – all you need is to be ready to step forward and grab that opportunity.

The first step is to reframe the idea of change in your mind. Rather than seeing it as something negative, perhaps scary, certainly uncomfortable, see it as something positive, an opportunity, an adventure. The second step is to remind yourself *why* you are making this change – because it will lead on to bigger and better things. Joining the Marines meant changing pretty much everything I had ever known, and as a result my eyes were opened up to opportunities that I could never have envisaged. The new situations I found myself in allowed me to grow and adapt in a powerful way. It's the same in life: if you can adapt to a new environment and embrace it, then good things will happen, and new opportunities will keep emerging on the horizon.

While stepping up and embracing change may seem like you are moving into a situation beyond your control, it's important to remember that you are still in charge of that change. In the Marines, we work extremely hard during our training to cultivate the mental edge required to engineer and master change. It is a game-changer with regards to our ability to cope with unexpected change or unfamiliar situations, along with any subsequent anxiety or pressure that may come with it. Yes, there are always aspects of any situation that you can't control, but what you *can* control is how you react. So if it feels as if that control is slipping away from you, pause, take that tactical knee, and assess your situation rationally. What are the elements that you *can* control? What are the elements that you can predict? Once you have established this, you can plot your route forward.

This openness to embracing change requires what's called a growth mindset – one that is not fixed and limited. The limited mind will be revealed by phrases such as 'I did my best but it wasn't meant to be', 'I guess it just wasn't for me' or 'I've taken this as far as I can'. This fixed way of thinking is often associated with blame, excuses or simply giving up. It's a mindset that is caught up in the past. In contrast, a growth mindset takes the lessons from past failures and uses them to adapt to the present and to make positive changes in future.

Recognising yourself

Adapting is all about a state of mind. The Royal Marines are renowned for their winning 'Commando mindset', which states: 'Be the first to understand, the first to adapt and respond, and the first to overcome.'

So adapting begins with understanding – both your situation and yourself. To cultivate a growth mindset, you will need to be at ease with yourself, embrace any flaws you may have and understand that hiding from any chinks in your armour means that you'll never overcome them. You need to be fully open when it comes to self-reflection and feel at ease in your own skin. This is a key element with regards to developing a growth mindset, because you remove the temptation to lie to yourself about where you are, where you want to be, and how you're going to get there. This can mean that, like Louis, you have to take stock, accept the place you find yourself in, and take the time to understand the path that brought you here.

In adapting and handling a pressurised situation in life, there is a need, every so often, to be honest with yourself and recognise your character, as certain personality traits can often lead to a certain pattern of response. When you accept how you're naturally inclined to handle a situation that could cause conflict or loss, then you can see that maybe that is not the best way to deal with every scenario and a different approach may be required.

Look back on the decisions you have made, the way you have previously reacted, the actions you have taken. Which were positive steps, and which set you back? And, crucially, what can you learn from both? When analysing a past event, a useful tip is to replace the word 'failing' with the word 'learning' and look at every challenge as an opportunity to learn. Changing your narrative like this can be beneficial in developing a growth mindset, as can incorporating the word 'yet' into your thinking: 'I haven't done it *yet* but I am working towards it . . .'

Once you have learned what you can from your path up to this point, you have to let it go. This is crucial. When cultivating adaptability in your life, it's important to face the situation you find yourself in and seek a way forward, no matter what has happened before. Regrets can have a huge effect on how you respond to change and can hold you back from getting your life back on track. Releasing and letting go of your regrets from the past is one of the keys to being able to move forward. If you're constantly looking back, you may miss opportunities that present themselves to you that could change your life for the better. It's impossible to change what you did in the past, so if it doesn't serve your purpose going forward, then just let it go. The only realistic option you have now is to choose to live in the present and prepare for the future. Maybe that means a complete change of direction, a clean break or embracing the skills you possess and using those to move forward.

My lifelong friend and former SBS (Special Boat Service) Colour Sergeant Tony 'Screwy' Driver found himself struggling to adapt to civilian life after leaving the Special Forces. Moving from such a high level of excellence, camaraderie and intensity, working alongside people of the same mindset, and then going into a normal job was never going to be easy, and it's a fact that some military personnel find adapting to civilian life difficult. When he found himself struggling in his new civilian job, Screwy took the time to recognise aspects of his own personality and put them in the context of his current situation, and he ultimately decided to leave, as the role just didn't suit him. As he eloquently explains: 'I went in to the boss and told him that I had to leave for the sake of my mental health – and for the physical welfare of the rest of his staff.'

Screwy went to live in Australia and, just like my mentor Louis, he can testify that it was the Marine values which allowed him to adapt and make a new life for himself on the other side of the world. This is how Screwy sums it up:

I was told that your mind will give up before your body will and that is so true, because the one thing harder than giving up is carrying on. Everyone asks themselves, 'Why am I doing this?' at some point in their lives, and the doubts about carrying on come in. The secret is to keep going until you find out why.

After military service, I did struggle a lot and had some dark moments. For most of my career, I was single-minded; my job was everything, and everything else came second, even relationships. Deciding to make such a massive change in my life by moving to the other side of the world, leaving family and friends, was very hard. I found that for me surfing was the key to keeping me in balance. I would have dark times, but getting out onto the water helped me to re-focus and kept me moving forward. That's why I would recommend strenuous exercise to anyone to keep the mind strong.

My resilience and state of mind to overcome hardship helped get me through the doubts and utter frustration of bouncing from one job to another before finally settling down – and I have to thank my amazing wife, Heidi, as well, because she has been a great support to me over the past ten years. It's easy to get into a rut, and that's why it's so important to adapt and to change. You have to be real with yourself and realise you just need to get up and do something – don't be afraid to change something in your life, no matter how small, and move forward, because you will survive and it can lead to something so much better.

As Screwy rightly highlights, adapting isn't just about forcing yourself to fit into a situation that doesn't work for you; it can also be about going out there and changing your circumstances, not just changing yourself.

Being the best version of yourself

Some adaptations are more extreme than others. One good friend of mine, JJ Chalmers, who you may have seen starring on *Strictly Come Dancing*, had to bring all his Marines training to the fore after he suffered serious facial, leg and arm injuries during a mission in Afghanistan. He had been selected to go into a Taliban compound to seek out a bomb-making factory. JJ loved being a Marine and felt honoured, at only twenty-three years of age, to have been selected for the mission. He and his team successfully located the factory, but

Me on my Green Beret presentation day, 1987.

Harry and Edie Mills, my grandparents and role models growing up.

With my mum and siblings

Lara Herbert and her troop completing their '30 miler' - the final commando test

My great friend, Commando Lara Herbert, and her troop completing their 'thirty miler', the final Commando training test.

Passing Out at the end of my Physical Training Instructor course,
one of the toughest courses in the Marines, 1998.

The Marines have taken me around the world. My first active tour was to Belfast in 1989. Back (L–R): me, Terry Barton, George Stephenson, Colin Hearn. Front (L–R): Rob Richardson, Shaun Noulton, Tony Callan (Sergeant).

'Capturing the Manifold Metering Station on the Al Faw Peninsula, Iraq', a painting of our entry into Iraq, 2003, by David Rowlands.

My wife Suzanne and children Charlie and Casey cheering us on in London as we attempt the World Record for Speed Marching, 2017.

My family – wife Suzanne and children Charlie, Sean, Marico and Casey – have always been my greatest source of support and inspiration.

We did it! Crossing the finish line and claiming our World Record.

At the United States Marine Corps Wounded Warrior Games in 2015 with (L–R) Al Le-Sueur, Lee Spencer, Andy Lock, Nick Goldsmith and Leigh Godwin.

(L–R) Harry Kane, Lee Spencer, Baz Barrett and myself at St George's Park, when Lee and Baz came to meet the England football team and share their own personal experiences of overcoming hardship. Our friendship has been one of the defining relationships of my life.

Lee Spencer, who didn't let losing a leg hold him back, completes his unsupported solo row across the Atlantic, breaking the able-bodied world record by an astonishing thirty-six days.

Me with Harry Kane (left) and Jermaine Defoe (right) on a training day with the England men's football team in the run-up to the 2018 World Cup. Jermaine described the Sheep Dip (opposite page) as 'like taking a penalty at the World Cup'.

© FA

With the whole England squad at the end of an exhausting training session. The words on the flag are the team's three core values – which we have blurred out as, understandably, they like to keep these private.

We put the England team through the grueling Marines endurance course, 2.5 miles of underwater obstacles and pitch-black, submerged tunnels. Here I am hauling Gareth Southgate out of the infamous 'Sheep Dip', an exercise in courage and trusting your teammates whom you rely on to pull you out of the submerged tunnel which is so narrow that once you enter you cannot move and you certainly couldn't swim out yourself.

From the endurance course to the couch on *Lorraine*, my career has taken me to many interesting places. Here I am with Lorraine Kelly, who first suggested that I write this book!

The Marines values helped me go places I had never dreamed of. Here I am with my wife, Suzanne, at Buckingham Palace in 2014.

In 2018 I was humbled and grateful to receive a Millies Award from *The Sun* for Inspiring Others, presented to me by Gareth Southgate.

One of the proudest moments of my life, and a moment to really pause and appreciate everything I have achieved, was being chosen to be a flag-bearer at the home Olympics, London 2012.

an Improvised Explosive Device went off, severely injuring JJ and killing two of his comrades. JJ's life was hanging by a thread, and it was only due to the quick thinking and courage of mutual friend Louis Nethercott and the others around him that he survived. His recovery took five years, and he still requires further surgery.

JJ's situation in life has changed dramatically. But drawing on his Marine training, he has not only adapted to his new situation, but has excelled within it. Adapting does not mean settling for second best, just because circumstances are less from ideal. Far from it. It means being the best possible version of yourself in any given situation. JJ knew that his circumstances do not define what he can achieve. Since his accident he has won a gold medal at the Invictus Games, become a television sports presenter for the BBC and starred on *Strictly Come Dancing*. This is how he explains that process of adapting:

With a little luck I survived that blast and then everything after that was down to the professionalism and courage of my brothers. Louis Nethercott saved my life and I would have done the same for him if I had to. Louis was on top of putting morphine into me and saving my life. Those first few moments in that chaotic scene were critical, because if they don't happen, then none of the rest happens, and I wouldn't have made it.

Lying in my hospital bed, I had gone from the peak of physical fitness to nothing. Life had changed instantly and that was a very hard thing to deal with mentally. As a Marine the training had honed and shaped me, teaching me to not listen to the demons in my head that told me to stop or that I couldn't do something. Now I was facing the ultimate test, because I was in horrendous pain and that didn't go away for a long time. I was still a Marine; my mind hadn't changed, but my body had.

I drew on my Marines training, which told me to take the next step. So, for me it was about the next minute, the next hour and day. I knew where I was, and now I had to unlock the idea that I was not going to stay there, I was going to challenge myself to adapt and go further in life. The physical adaptions were hard, but it was that step-by-step mindset that got me through to the Invictus Games, to compete in the recumbent cycling, to go on and do *Strictly*.

I have been fortunate that I have always been surrounded by guys who inspired me. The Royal Marines shaped me into the person I am, and the Invictus Games gave me and so many others a reason for getting out of bed – and for some to just keep living. I've had many say to me that without the Invictus Games they would have killed themselves.

The Royal Marines is all about being the best version of yourself, and that sometimes means you have to adapt. After that IED went off, I no longer had a career in the Royal Marines, but I was still a Royal Marine in my mind. I could still be the best version of myself.

I find it really poignant that when JJ talks about being the best version of himself, he doesn't add any caveats or excuses, no allowance for circumstances that might get in the way of that. In other words, wherever you find yourself *today*, you can be the best version of yourself and take yourself forward from there, because you have the value of adaptability. You could be at the summit, the bottom or somewhere in between, and despite the circumstances there is always an opportunity to adapt and move forward.

Teachability is the next level up from ability

In order to cultivate the skill of adaptability, there are certain things we have to put aside. One of these is the belief that you know best. I have seen many people with an incredible amount of talent who have wasted it through their inability to listen to the counsel of others. Some think they 'have all the answers', and this type of attitude is linked to a fixed mindset where the rate of personal growth is slow. Those with talent are often overtaken by those with the right attitude. This came to real focus for one young officer whom I was working alongside in training, shortly after my return from Iraq.

Part of my role as a senior NCO was to guide this 21-year-old as he learned what it meant to be an officer. During one particular exercise, the enemy was inside a farm complex and we had to decide how we were going to attack them. We were all fitted with sensors on our kit and our weapons had special laser mechanisms so when we got hit it would register. The young officer in question was leading the exercise. I gave my advice, which he didn't listen to, and then he made his decision. He was a smart young man, but my experience told me that his judgement was incorrect. I gave him one last chance to change his mind and consider the option I laid before him. He insisted he had made his decision and that the attack would go ahead as he had planned.

So, we carried out the orders and all thirty men were 'killed' within minutes. It was like blowing the whistle for the men to go over the top at the Somme. Luckily this was just a training exercise. That young man and I had to have a serious chat afterwards, and we spoke about the importance of having a flexible mind that could listen and take on board the input of others, especially those with more experience than he had. We turned it into an open conversation where he could learn. The way to maximise your potential is to demonstrate that you are someone who listens and has a willingness to become teachable. Teachability is the next level up from ability, as any top sporting coach will tell you.

Talent alone is rarely enough, so remember to take any criticism as feedback and accept that *all* feedback is positive – no matter how painful it may be to listen to. While setbacks are painful, the pain of failure is only temporary. Listen and learn from others and keep in mind that if you don't try, then you fail 100 per cent of the time. It is often the case that people who form a growth mindset often go on to acquire a greater sense of purpose and lead successful lives. That young officer has gone on to have a very successful career, and when we meet every so often, we recall that day with a wry smile and how much it taught him.

So welcome feedback, listen to others, and keep challenging yourself to learn. Ask yourself key questions along the way, such as: 'What did I learn today?' and 'How could I have done it differently?' and 'What kept me going?' These will help you assess your performance and allow you to be open and honest about how you can change for the better. In reality, life is just one long learning process that is constantly requiring you to adapt in large or small ways.

Never stop adapting

It's one thing understanding another point of view and quite another to have the humility to then change course, adapt your thinking and choose a different way. This can be particularly tough for parents or those in leadership roles across sport or business, because pride and ego can block the way, especially for those in positions of responsibility who may feel the pressure to always be right.

For those who have more experience, who might find themselves in positions of responsibility, the ability to adapt is crucial in being able to promote continuous change and drive improvements in their teams. This might mean demonstrating a wider understanding of the circumstances surrounding a certain situation and how they can adapt a company or team for the better – and this is an area where everyone's voice is important. While it's important to listen to those who are senior to you (in rank, or age, or experience), it is also important to be open to ideas that come from those junior to you. We all have a voice and, as we increasingly see, our young people are willing and able to vocalise their thoughts and ideas.

When you create an open environment where others are free to express themselves and where people are listened to by their boss, your employees are more likely to contribute to its growth with innovation and ideas. Having worked with many young people, I've always found their observations to be instructive and full of innovation. We must nurture this, and listen to their opinions and points of view, because there is so much that we can learn from the next generation.

So, the value of adapting is not just about the growth and development of young people, it is something that continues throughout your career, throughout your life. Even if you are at the summit of your profession, it doesn't mean you stop adapting. The Marines know this, and there are specifically tailored leadership courses at every single level, from recruit to general, that teach you the lessons that you need to be able to adapt and grow into every new position.

Decompression

As an organisation, the Royal Marines has had to adapt and change over the years, although its core values have remained the same. There is no doubt that the Corps has become much more aware of the effects that the battlefield can have on a person. The intensity of being on tour, of having to adapt to a new harsh environment and carry out missions with a group of guys that have your back, with lives on the line, has a great impact.

It used to be that men and women would return home straight from the battlefield to their homes, back into normal family life, and often it didn't work out too well for their loved ones. Some could switch off from the battlefield mentality right away, but others found it harder to acclimatise, and so the Marines decided something had to change.

To allow the Marines to adapt back into family life, it was decided that there should be what was called a 'decompression' period of a couple of days. For me, on my return from Afghanistan, that was forty-eight hours in Cyprus. There we were able to release all the pressure that naturally builds up over the course of a tour of duty. We could share stories and generally take some time to disengage from the combat zone before returning to normal life. Decompression improves your mood and reduces the chance of mental health deterioration.

This principle of decompression is one that I believe is needed in daily life. For the one-parent family trying to make ends meet, the boss trying to keep the business afloat and their workers in jobs, or the student dealing with the high level of stress around exams, a time for decompression is critical – and could even be life-saving. We are all too aware of the shocking rise in suicides and the dramatic rise in mental health issues in the population overall, and often it is because people cannot find a release – or they seek a release in substances that sadly only lead to an increase in problems, such as addiction or depression.

As individuals, we all need to find time to regularly decompress. I recognise that that might be easier said than done but getting into a stringent routine of decompression really is crucial, otherwise we find ourselves weighed down with life's pressures without even realising how we got to such a vulnerable situation. What this routine looks like will be individual to you. It could be a walk in the park, maybe a bus journey, a short train ride or signing up to your local park run – anything that removes you from your pressurised situation so that you are recharged for the following day's challenges. Making the time to exercise is a great way to decompress at the end of a busy day and obviously has its own health benefits.

Home can also be a place of decompression. It should, if possible, be viewed as a sanctuary from all the pressures of work. (This isn't always practical, of course, especially if you have kids at home and a million jobs still to do there.) Take small but critical steps to try and protect this space. Try to leave your work at the office and not bring it home: turn off your laptop, do not check your emails and stop work-related communication until the next day. This can help you put aside any impending deadlines and will enable you to be fresh and clear-headed when you return to work the following morning, because you have decompressed from the previous day's challenges.

The need to adapt is something we will all face – and something we *should* face. It is key to growing and developing as an individual, enabling us to embrace new experiences and truly get the best out of life. But allow yourself a little decompression time too – you've earned it.

CHAPTER 5: ADAPTABILITY LESSON SUMMARY

Remember . . .

- You can't control your environment, but you can control how you react and adapt to it.
- Convert life's setbacks into your future success.
- Develop the growth mindset and mental edge that is required to master innovation and engineer change.

Step 1 – WHAT is adaptability?

Adaptability is your ability to modify your ideas or behaviours to make them suitable to a new situation. It describes how open you are to embracing new concepts and how you respond to change. People with high adaptability are often flexible people who adopt an open growth mindset.

Step 2 – WHY is adaptability important?

Change is one of the unquestionable constants in everyone's life. It is important to learn how to adapt and embrace change in your life, otherwise you can find yourself stuck, stagnating or left behind and you will miss out on many of the opportunities life has to offer. Your ability to adapt will be crucial to keeping you moving forwards and will lead to personal and professional growth and success.

Step 3 – HOW to become adaptable in your life?

+ Accept and believe that things change – often for the better.
+ Expect the unexpected and become accustomed to uncertainty.
+ Be willing to try new things to get a different outcome.
+ Keep learning – people who continually learn tend to thrive and adapt better in any given situation.
+ When having to adapt to extreme change, build in decompression time for processing and adjustment.

CHAPTER 6

Courage

Definition:
Physical – The ability to control your fear in
a dangerous or difficult situation.
Moral – The ability to do the right thing
despite external pressure or opposition.

When you ask a Royal Marine what it takes to be part of the UK's Commando Green Beret amphibious fighting force, they will immediately mention 'courage'. And believe me: when you face formidable enemies such as the IRA, the Iraqi Special Forces and the Taliban, you need that quality in abundance.

It was certainly required when I arrived in Belfast for my first operational tour as a young, inexperienced Royal Marine with Lima Company, 42 Commando, in March 1988. At the time, newspapers and TV channels were dominated by the shocking murders of Corporals Derek Woods and David Howes of the Royal Signals. After straying into the path of an IRA funeral cortege, they had been dragged from their car, beaten and disarmed, before being stripped and beaten again and then finally shot dead in an act of savage brutality. So as we set foot on the streets of Belfast, we were all too aware of what this enemy was capable of. This became even more apparent when we were sat down and shown the uncensored footage – so gruesome that it had not been transmitted to the public.

As we patrolled the streets of a Republican area of Belfast, an incident began to unfold that inescapably brought those images to my mind. My team commander, Lance Corporal Peter 'Louis' Lewis, was leading the patrol. He was a man of great integrity and courage, and a leader who always had the backs of his men. As a team, we knew that Louis would sacrifice himself for us without a second's thought, and I reckon that went both ways. Now, however, it was he who had found himself in real danger.

We were in the heart of the New Lodge area of Belfast, a stronghold of the IRA, and Louis had got into a fracas with a few of the locals. At first there were ten or so around him. Within seconds, ten became twenty. With the horrific death of those corporals fresh in our minds, I had a real sense of foreboding that this situation could go the same way. Suddenly the door behind Louis opened and the mob tried to grab him around the neck and drag him backwards into one of the houses. They were trying to snatch him, and our four-man team knew that if they got him into the house and we lost sight of him, he would probably suffer the same fate as Derek Woods and David Howes.

There was no way I was going let the enemy take my hero Louis, for him to become just another victim of the Troubles. Maybe I lost it a bit, but I'd like to think there was courage behind our actions as well. A rage came about me the likes of which I had not experienced before, and with no regard for our own safety, myself and Robbo (another member of our patrol) charged headfirst straight into the mob towards Louis. The boss broke free and we got him out of there as fast as we could.

It is important to note at this point that courage should not be confused with recklessness. Ironically, Louis was annoyed with us for putting the team in what could have become an even more volatile situation, but there was simply no question that we could have acted differently; we would have done anything to stop him from being taken. We did not act without thinking, however. Courage isn't just about acting even when you are afraid, but it is about taking *calculated* risks, so sometimes it helps to remove the emotion completely from a situation. It is all too easy to make knee-jerk instant reactions in the heat of a moment, but showing courage sometimes requires you to hold your nerve in tough situations and ensure that you are making the best choices even under enormous pressure.

Selfless courage, the action triggered by a need to help someone else regardless of personal cost, is one of the biggest reasons I stayed in the Royal Marines. A frequent question put to me is: 'How many people have you killed?', and I always respond with the question I would rather answer but have never been asked, which is 'How many lives have you saved?' I give that reply because that is the reason I did the job; the duty of the Royal Marines is above all to protect, and I know we have saved a lot of lives over the years of our existence and that to do so we have often had to display huge amounts of courage, often putting our own lives on the line to save others. We value the lives of our fellow brothers and sisters in the Marines and those of the people we vow to safeguard, and while this same core value is not evident in some of the enemy forces that we have faced, I believe that it takes more, not less courage to put your life on the line for one another when life itself is valued. We know what we stand to lose, so there will always be an element of fear, and it takes courage to go forward in the face of that.

Physical courage of the kind we demonstrated in Belfast that day can be part of your DNA. We had only a split-second to react – fight, flight or freeze – and that inner courage rose to the situation. In truth, however, I think there is more to courage than this, and that it is also a skill that can be learned. You may not feel inherently courageous, but it is something you can grow and nurture – and we will look at how to do so later in the chapter – then, finally, when you are faced with a situation that tests it, you will discover the true extent of your own courage.

Facing fears

We are all called upon to show courage at some point in our lives. It may be moral courage, or it may be physical courage, but both ultimately stem from the same place: facing up to fear. It may not be as dramatic as being a target of the IRA or an enemy sniper. You might be under the cosh of a bully at work, you may be afraid to take a risk, or a fear of failure in your life may have gripped you. It may be a fear that manifests in the form of pressure, whether that comes from others or yourself.

No matter the situation, when it comes to building a courageous mindset, the first step is to accept and face your fears, as avoiding them only makes them more intense and intimidating. Some people and organisations will link emotion and vulnerability to a sense of weakness, and so our natural instinct is to quell them. However, suppressing negative feelings will only feed your fears, thereby strengthening them. Only by exposing yourself to your fears can you make it easier to face them.

Former Marine turned top civil servant Dan O'Mahoney is someone who has enough courage to speak openly about his fears and believes that it is in pointing to them that courage is allowed to blossom. As he explains:

I think I see courage slightly differently to others. So, if you can jump out of helicopters and not be scared, that's great – but for me it is not courage. Courage, for me, is being terrified of something and confronting it. I've spent most of the past fifteen years in the civil service terrified I would get 'found out', pushing myself to take opportunities and not knowing if I could do the job or not. For my first eight years in the civil service, I had low-level panic attacks from the moment I would get up to the point I would go to sleep. How do you keep going when under that amount of anxiety? It's down to courage – it's that Marines value of putting one foot in front of the other. When I left the Marines, I felt scared a lot; I had a fear of failure. But I took myself back to my time in the Marines when we were doing mountain training and I was terrified because I suddenly realised that I was afraid of heights. Courage is being scared and doing it anyway, and that's how I got through mountain training. Sometimes in life that's just the way it has to be.

Dan succinctly describes the moments of doubt and fear that can sit alongside courage and how, at those points, there is a decision to be made – whether to step forward and courageously walk through the fear or remain where you are.

My late great friend and former Marine Terry Barton was someone who I knew would never take a step back. Even in the most trying of circumstances, he would taking five steps forward before I'd even thought about a first. When I consider feats of raw courage, I immediately think of him.

Terry was awarded a richly deserved commendation for bravery during a tour of Belfast following an incident in which he literally saved lives, all due to his seemingly instinctive courage in the face of extreme danger. He was patrolling as part of a team in a hard Republican area of Belfast called Ardoyne when a man came out of nowhere swinging a machete, looking to kill or maim the patrol. Terry didn't blink. He went straight towards the man and shot a baton round which disabled the attacker, saving the life of an RUC man who was on patrol with him, along with the other Marines at his side. And this wasn't a one-off act of courage; Terry personified this value and lived it daily. Sadly, he died in 2019 of a brain tumour, but not before we had the chance to talk about old times and to share some laughs with fellow Marine and former Corps Regiment Sergeant Major (RSM) Phil Gilby. He was a wonderful man, and I not only had the honour of giving the eulogy at his funeral, but got to take his sons to an England game, where I introduced them to the Liverpool captain and England player Jordan Henderson. That would have meant a lot to Terry, because he was a massive lifelong Liverpool fan.

The many forms of courage

Courage comes to the fore in different ways. One of the most difficult situations is when moral courage is required to stand up to others. The bully you face may not threaten a knee-capping or the murder of a loved one, as with the IRA, they may simply insinuate that it's their way or the highway. That could mean a roadblock in regard to promotion, or it might be constant online abuse and mockery, whether privately or in full view of peers. Whatever form it takes – whether it's in the family unit, the workplace, the sports field, in school or on the street corner – make no mistake: bullying wrecks lives. Preserving your integrity, dignity and honour will at some point require you to have the courage to stand up for what you know is right.

This is not always easy but, in my experience, when you

see something that is wrong, you must act to do the right thing and not simply take the easiest route. This is a form of moral courage. If you're ever unsure of how to handle certain people or situations, speak to someone you feel comfortable with. Then, trust your instincts and act positively. This will build your self-assurance, and it won't be as intimidating the next time when you are required to summon some courage from within.

Then there is courage in the face of failure, something that we have already touched upon in earlier chapters. After a defeat, the easy option is to slump into a mindset that the world is against you and whatever you try will just end in failure – that the world can only offer less than what you want in life. But real courage consumes past failures with an unquenchable thirst to go again and again and again. Courage is required to own up to mistakes, to personal failings. In doing that, by exposing your vulnerabilities and facing your fears, you set yourself free to be even more courageous in life. Publicly facing up to your failures – and overcoming them – requires a huge amount of courage and is an important aspect of leadership. A strong leader will not try to hide their failings but will have the courage to use those failings to encourage and inspire their team.

This is something that I encountered when working with the England football team. Gareth Southgate has worked diligently to make sure that his players realise that it is all right to fail, because it doesn't mean you are a failure. It just means that you are on a journey and that failing is just one part of the process of growing and moving forwards.

I was privileged to be there when Gareth opened up

about his own vulnerabilities and how he had to face up to his missed penalty during the semi-final of Euro '96 against Germany. I was at Wembley that day, and the dream of England reaching a major final for the first time in thirty years ended when he missed that 12-yard kick.

He would openly admit that the pain burned for some time but, ultimately, he had to make sure it didn't mean the end of his football journey. He explained to his players how he went to a pretty dark place because of what happened. That expression of vulnerability required courage, and it paid off, creating a greater bond with the men he was now leading. They respected his openness and saw this as a demonstration of courage from a true leader – and so did I.

Frankly, we need more leaders with this kind of moral courage right across society. Today's generation is different from the previous one, and expressing your feelings is a more accepted part of modern-day life. By showing others that it's OK to share your vulnerabilities, you are in effect giving them permission to do the same, and they are likely to feel more open to express their weaknesses with a view to improving their own lives. People who are prepared to share such life experiences allow others to see deep inside and uncover what lies beneath. You may feel very exposed, but sharing your vulnerabilities is a form of bravery that requires real moral courage.

Growing courage

As with all the values we have looked at in this book, courage is something to be worked at. It isn't some magic dust that just falls on one person and not another. Courage is a habit, something you can learn. Most of us are not born fearless, so we shouldn't expect to miraculously be courageous by nature. The opportunity to develop courage will be there for us all, however. The question of how to perform under pressure will present itself at some point, whether in elite sport, in the classroom, at home or the workplace.

The first thing to ensure is that you have been practising courage, putting yourself in situations where a small amount of courage is required. At first this is just about stepping slightly outside of your comfort zone. This might make you feel nervous, but it's a highly effective way to develop courage incrementally. The more you are exposed to an unfamiliar environment or situation, the less intimidating it becomes and the more your courage grows. Taking those firsts steps, however small, is pivotal to help you to thrive in an unfamiliar environment when the pressure is on. As you put yourself in these situations, bear in mind Dan O'Mahoney's key point about 'being scared and doing it anyway' – remember that you have *chosen* to do this, you are in control. This will give you a greater sense of autonomy, which will in turn allow you to cope should anything unexpected occur, which is where fear often originates from.

This is how my good friend Dr Lara Herbert describes this incremental growth of courage:

Courage is the decision to act and do what you think is right, despite being afraid and knowing the odds are against you. I think it stems from personal values and comes from deep within, but can most definitely be nurtured by cultural values too, i.e. if the organisation within which you work truly values acts of courage and selflessness. If these acts are recognised and commended, newcomers then have examples and role models to look up to and the effect self-perpetuates. It can also be developed by exposure to incremental risk in a supported way, such as through adventurous training or within the workplace, for example being encouraged to perform tasks above your level, but within your ability.

For me, the most striking example of courage in combat was that displayed by the assistant medics in Helmand Province, Afghanistan. Most of these individuals were not Commando-trained and they had never been to war. Most had not even done much land-based training for war before. Some had come from ships, some from submarines and some from administrative jobs in hospitals in the UK, but these medics went out on daily Royal Marine-led foot and vehicle patrols to provide point-of-injury care. They were fully aware of the risks they were taking, as they had undergone medical training to prepare for major trauma and they were rotated between the Forward Operating Bases and Bastion Hospital, so had seen devastating war injuries.

The medics I worked with carried out their roles with enormous pride. Despite being in completely unfamiliar environments and often fearing for their own safety, they carried out their duties with professionalism and calm.

They reflected deeply after difficult days and took much
more than they needed to heart.

Lara makes an interesting point about developing courage in
an incremental way specifically in the context of exposing
yourself to levels of risk. As we discussed at the outset of the
chapter, courage is also about risk management. You don't have
to jump in at the deep end; you can grow your courage one
step at a time. As Lara puts it, 'perform tasks above your level,
but within your ability'. When practising courage, you want
to stretch yourself without putting yourself in situations that
are likely to overwhelm you. So if you struggle with public
speaking, for example, a very common fear, this might mean
putting yourself forward to do a presentation at work. You
needn't jump straight in at the deep end with a speech to 1,000
people, or an all-company presentation – start small, present
to your team, take every opportunity to speak up in meetings,
and expand your comfort zone, relentlessly, step by step.

Over the years, I've been exposed to a variety of adventurous activities that have been both exhilarating and
challenging, and which have supported me in my personal
and professional growth. Often, this has involved stepping
outside of my comfort zone. I am not someone who is naturally comfortable with heights – a common fear – but through
progressive exposure to height (such as high-rope courses,
helicopter abseiling, rock climbing and parachuting), I have
learned to live with it. The key here is that I have exposed
myself to something I am afraid of, but within a controlled
environment. This means that if I later find myself in a
risky situation that involves heights, I already have a bank of

courage to draw upon. I have familiarised myself with the courage needed to deal with the situation.

Often, growing levels of courage in this controlled way can help you to become a more courageous person in other areas of your life. The ability to balance risk and courage, to keep a cool head and maintain control of the situation, is a transferable skill that will spill over into other areas of your life. Practising courage works, and the confidence you gain from such experiences breeds self-confidence and self-belief.

The fruits/rewards of courage

It takes courage to live out the life you desire. There will be moments when the road is tough, but nothing worth having is ever easy to attain.

So, what is it that's standing in the way of YOUR dreams, ambitions and goals? Most of the time it may not be clear to you what's holding you back. In most cases, however, it's fear. Fear of failure, fear of loss, fear of the unknown – all will require courage to overcome them. But, as we have said, you can vanquish your fears by accepting them and then taking them on, step by step, building experiences that require you to demonstrate some form of courage. The key is to push through even when you feel scared and unsure of the outcome. Don't become results-focused; just narrow your view to being brave enough to do the right thing, and success will follow. One of the most important aspects of being brave is knowing that, somewhere inside of you, courage will be there when you need it most.

Like the other values discussed so far, courage can become a part of who you are. It can form part of your central beliefs and character, and become something that you draw upon day after day, month after month. And over time, that elevated level of courage you worked so hard to achieve becomes your new normal. This was the case for a young female army private I once knew whose job it was to drive a tanker full of highly volatile fuel to every Forward Operating Base every week for six months through Helmand Valley in Afghanistan – one of the most dangerous places in the world. As part of our well-trained Commando Logistical Unit, her role was critical to resupply Marines at operating bases further forward. She was under constant threat of attack by IEDs from the Taliban, as the tanker presented a huge and highly valued target for enemy forces. Yet, despite that, she summoned the inner courage to do this perilous job day in, day out without a single word of complaint. Six months is an incredibly long time to repeatedly demonstrate courage under extreme pressure, and she never wavered once.

Sometimes in life you can feel as if you're hanging on by the skin of your teeth, that there is no end to the darkness – maybe that failure is coming down the track once again. Sometimes courage is needed to just keep putting one foot in front of the other, just to get through the next day. But, if you're still hanging on, then you're still practising courage, and that means that as that courage grows, you will have the chance to move forward. From there, the sky is the limit, and you will see what can be achieved when you are fuelled by that undeniable courage and will to succeed. The best things in life lie just the other side of your darkest fears.

CHAPTER 6: COURAGE LESSON SUMMARY

Remember ...

* Become courageous by facing your fears, but remember that courage is not the same as recklessness.
* Courage comes in many forms and can be quiet and understated.
* The best things in life lie just the other side of your darkest fears.

Step 1 – WHAT is courage?

Physical courage is about being fearful yet choosing to act bravely in a dangerous or difficult situation.

Moral courage is about making a personal choice to do the right thing and not the thing that is easiest.

Step 2 – WHY is courage important?

Fear is one of the most debilitating emotions that will hold you back in life. Courage does not mean getting rid of fear, but it does mean facing up to that fear and pushing through it with confidence. This will enable you to take huge steps forward in your life and grasp opportunities you would otherwise have allowed to pass by. This type of courage is a gamechanger in the way you think and act. It's how impossible dreams are fulfilled.

Step 3 – 'How' to become more COURAGEOUS in your life.

- Courage is a habit you can learn.
- Courage grows one small step at a time.
- Always take the initiative to face your fears head on and you can do so in a controlled and positive way.
- Possess the courage to do the things that others won't do, to have the success that others won't have.
- Think big, aim high and always do the right thing.

CHAPTER 7

Kindness

Definition: The quality of being friendly, generous or considerate.

A mother and father were preparing to welcome home their son from a six-month tour of Afghanistan and it was my solemn duty on a bright summer's day to inform them that their son had been shot and killed while serving his country. This was not the first time during my thirty-two-year career that I had conducted this difficult task as part of my role as a Royal Marines officer.

I got the call to go to the family home, an hour's drive from central London. I knew they would probably be allowing themselves to believe that their son had made it through the tour unscathed, as he was due home in just a couple of days. There are strict procedures to follow in such an instance, including only telling the nominated emergency contact first, and in this case it was his mum. Before breaking the news, you do a drive-by to assess the scene. I sat and stared at the steps of the house, and had the chilling thought, *This could be someone coming to my wife one day, to give her the same news.*

When I got to the top of the five steps, I rang the doorbell. The door had that frosted glass effect, so I could see someone coming towards me, a blurred, bouncing ball of light, skipping merrily down the hallway. She opened the door and beamed up at me, and I said, 'Are you X, the mother of marine Y?' She just screamed 'Marines' and fell backwards. I rushed in and caught her as she fainted, just in time to stop her hitting her head.

I know it wasn't my fault, but I can't help but feel that I was responsible for taking the light out of that lady's eyes. Afterwards, I had to go to a local pub for a large whiskey. I know I'm mentally strong – you have to be as a Marine – but that was very, very hard and still affects me to this day. It hurts deeply because we really do care.

Kindness may not be what springs to mind when considering what it is to be a Marine, but I can assure you that it is another crucial value. Yes, we are a fearsome fighting force, but kindness runs parallel with the job we have to do, and it is a value that can easily be overlooked in our fast-paced, operationally driven world. But without kindness, many of the other core values crumble. Respect, courage, understanding, integrity – they all have a core of kindness.

It is always heart-warming to observe people who go out of their way to be kind towards others, who don't discriminate, and who radiate kindness in everything they do. These are the types of people who show empathy and caring for others, and tend to look out for those in need around them, following up and acting in a supportive way. It takes effort to be kind; it's a lot easier to do nothing and not be sympathetic to the suffering of others. Even a small act of kindness can go a very long way, however, and can blossom into something very big. And the act of giving brings its own rewards; I've seen first-hand how it can grow communities, strengthen relationships and build mutual respect.

The importance of kindness

In the Marines, kindness needs to be at the fore, just as I believe it should be in life. My great friend and former Royal Marines officer Jock Hutchinson is a straight-talking Scot, and although his rough edges might not immediately suggest it, kindness is one of his core values. For the past decade he has been running an incredible project in Scotland called Horseback UK, which uses equine therapy to help injured servicemen and women who are physically and mentally broken towards recovery and a better life. As Jock points out, it was the Marines' value of kindness that gave him the desire to make a difference to the lives of his 'brothers and sisters':

Kindness is everything. You need it to be able to truly understand other human beings. There is no doubt that the Marines are brilliant at killing people and they have enabled people to go into battle and achieve incredible feats to keep our country safe. But to make me the person I needed to be, they indoctrinated me with a set of values that enabled to me to properly interact with the rest of the world. People are happier when they have a set of parameters in which to operate, to be a good human being, and there is no doubt that the Marines instilled this in every recruit, and kindness was a clear value that had to be developed and seen in practice. Leadership is based on empathy – or should be based on empathy – because leaders, as we were taught in the Marines, are there to bring the best out in you and to take you to levels you never thought possible.

The Marines have a great ability to take people from every background and mesh them together into a band of brothers, and they do it through the values they demand from everyone. You are what you are taught to be. We often seem to have forgotten that it is our connection with other people, that sense of community, that makes us who we are. I remember a mother coming up to me and asking, 'What have you done to my son? He's transformed!' The Marines had given him a set of values and purpose, and he bought into it, embracing the camaraderie and becoming a better person. You can't do that without kindness.

I too believe that kindness is at the root of human connection. It shows in the way that we feel an attraction toward and cherish acts of kindness. This is something that humans have a deep capacity for, especially when the chips are down. I can think of many times around the world when I have seen people showing astonishing levels of kindness even when consumed by fear, loss or grief. And I'm sure we can all think of countless examples from recent times, of kindness shown by health and care workers on the pandemic front lines, and by friends and families going the extra mile to stay in touch with loved ones during lockdowns.

How to exercise kindness

Kindness is seen through actions, through looking out for each other, either physically or emotionally, in big ways and small. We can show kindness to family and friends, to people we know and love, or to strangers. As we moved around south London during my primary school years, I remember being the new lad at a new school on so many occasions, facing the fear and trepidation of the unknown. Humans are naturally less likely to be kind to people we don't know. On each occasion, I remember those who were kind enough to say hello and speak to the new boy. You remember kindness, and the people who showed it, because they have a real and positive impact on you and your mental health.

Kindness in the Marines, as I'm sure you would expect, is not about chocolates and rose petals on your pillow, but it is a value that runs deeply through our own Corps family. Importantly for us, it also extends into our wider Corps family, friends and supporters who are scattered around the world in every walk of life. Building connections with people who are far away has never been easier. In today's world, where we can interact with others in a micro-second, it only takes five minutes to reach out to someone you know and check in on them. Letting people know that you are thinking of them maintains and strengthens relationships, no matter how far away they might be. Kindness doesn't recognise boundaries or excuses, and if you really care for someone, then remind yourself why they are special and go out of your way to keep in touch.

Being kind to strangers is another thing altogether and says everything about your inner value and belief system. It's the polar opposite of the indiscriminate hatred that we sometimes see in the world, and I know that we can change the world around us for the better by showing more compassion than hate. I really think it's that simple. A warm smile on a cold day, a helping hand with the shopping, a friendly waitress – each positive interaction can alter the vector of someone's day.

Persistent kindness

We have talked about the value of determination earlier in the book, and this comes into play in kindness, too. Kindness doesn't give up, even if it is unreciprocated or difficult or doesn't appear to be having any effect. Kindness is as tenacious as a Marine.

Prince Harry was one who demonstrated the value of persistent kindness in abundance. He was very well thought of in the Marines and personally invested much of his time and effort into our wounded, injured and sick ranks of Hasler Company, a multidisciplinary unit that I commanded and which was responsible for the recovery and care of our most complex, seriously injured and long-term ill soldiers, sailors, airmen and Marines. These were men and women from very different backgrounds but who had a common bond of service, and Prince Harry – just like his mother Princess Diana – had a great way of making people feel at ease, to the point where many of them could have been forgiven for entirely forgetting his royal status.

Prince Harry's work in the development of the Invictus Games speaks for itself and has left a great legacy across the world. The Games are a multi-sport event for those military personnel who have been injured or wounded and it has had a huge impact on those who have had to battle back from the trauma of warfare and loss. As the Commanding Officer of Hasler Company, I saw first-hand how adaptive sport and the Invictus Games inspired so many on their journey to recovery. They were back representing their nation with pride. It gave them new goals and made them realise they were still highly capable members of our Armed Forces.

One man for whom Invictus played a crucial role in his journey was a young Marine called Louis Nethercott, one of those who had saved JJ Chalmers's life. It has been well documented in the media that Louis suffered very badly from Post-Traumatic Stress Disorder, which is a horrible blight on many of those who have served their country. Indeed, it is a grim fact that more Falklands veterans have died through suicide than lost their lives in the conflict.

Louis suffered from PTSD due to what he had experienced and seen during his service in Afghanistan. Louis would describe to me how he could be fine one day but was unable to plan anything for the next twenty-four hours because he simply didn't know what tomorrow would bring.

Sometimes, he could be up all night without any sleep, tortured by PTSD. It affects people in different ways and it's just horrendous to see.

But this is when the kindness and comradeship of the Royal Marines came to the fore. The team at Hasler Company worked with Louis for years, often going two steps forward and one back as we sought to help him as best we could. Two very senior Marines in particular, Jim and Marty, really went the extra mile when it came to the depth of support and care they gave, and it paid off in an amazing way in the friendships and respect that ensued.

In 2016 in Orlando, Florida, at the opening ceremony of the second Invictus Games, Louis Nethercott stood there with JJ Chalmers, his fellow Marine whose life Louis saved, by his side. They were flanked by Prince Harry, former US President George W. Bush and Oscar-winning actor Morgan Freeman, as they addressed the crowd, in front of TV cameras with the world looking on, telling their story and what the event meant to them.

The persistent kindness in action of their support team, relentlessly practised over many years, sometimes met without thanks, sometimes with overwhelming gratitude, had brought both these men to this point. That's a challenge for all of us in life – not only what act of kindness will we do to make a difference, but how much determination and drive will we bring to that kindness? Because that's when you start to see that kindness can have such a powerful and lasting reaction. So, you can implement kindness right now, but you must also make it part of your daily routine.

Invisible kindness

Kindness also doesn't ask for recognition. I have seen this time and again in my time in the Marines. A country that has shown me and my fellow Marines boundless kindness is America. The Invictus Games were born out of the Wounded Warrior Games organised by the American Marines and I have to say that every time we went to the States we were treated like kings. The generosity and kindness shown to us knew no bounds.

Sitting at a restaurant with my fellow Royal Marines in Oceanside, California during the Wounded Warrior Games, a jumble of prosthetic arms and legs all piled up on an adjacent table, I offered to pay for the lads and was calculating that the meal and copious amount of alcohol was going to hit my credit card to the tune of around 2,000 dollars. But when I asked for the bill – after taking a deep breath – I was told that it had already been taken care of. Obviously bewildered, I asked 'By whom?' It turned out that a US Marine Corps general had been sitting across from us with his wife; he had decided to pay for our night out and then quietly slipped away without saying a word. I rushed out to thank him but he was already gone.

It was a clear example of how invisible acts of kindness are so potent because they don't benefit the giver in any way. They are not driven by personal gain and are offered in a way that is completely selfless. Invisible acts don't need to be seen to be appreciated, and sometimes aren't consciously noticed at all – but they will always have an impact. In fact, it is the anonymous acts that carry the most weight; both humane and

noble in their nature, they are devoid of ego and are intoxicating in nature. That type of comradeship and kindness
among Marines stretches right across the world. Having met
fellow Marine brothers and sisters across all continents who
were representing their own nations at the Wounded Warrior
Games, there is clearly a huge mutual respect and we felt that
in a very special way that night – and my credit card didn't
have to take a beating!

As you go about your daily life, be alert to the potential
for invisible acts of kindness. And if you see an opportunity,
don't hesitate – act.

Kindness in the face of unkindness

One of the most difficult times to show kindness is when it is
not reciprocated, or, indeed, when it is met with unkindness
or even hatred. Showing kindness and compassion to those
who do not return it, even to the enemy, reflects the standards
and values of the Marines.

As I have said, I regard myself as a peaceful warrior and
that cuts across how our enemies would like us to be perceived. This was evident in Northern Ireland during my
two tours during the Troubles, when engaging with the
IRA and patrolling streets in which we knew the enemy had
painted us in a certain light. It was clear to me that those in
the community in Belfast were mentally and emotionally
exhausted by the Troubles by the late 1980s and onwards.
The people we met there were just like any other group in
the world: when they saw how we operated professionally

and understood that we were there to protect and serve them, they responded in a positive way. Small acts of basic human kindness, like handing out sweets to kids or helping someone in distress, were recognised, and on occasion even led to little pieces of intelligence and information, which sometimes saved lives. That wasn't the motivation behind these acts of kindness, but it does go to show something about the value of kindness, which can sometimes be disregarded in a world that often pushes the narrative that to get on in life you have to look after number one and trample over others. I simply don't believe that is the case, and from my experiences I have noticed that good things generally happen to nice people. One of the effects of being kind is that people are mostly kind back to you, and when you exhibit selflessness, when you look out for and show a genuine heartfelt care for others, that engenders high levels of trust and respect. It becomes contagious.

My great friend, US Marine Corps Sergeant Major Michael Mack relayed a poignant story of how he found himself in a position of educating a couple of his young recruits in regard to what kindness is after the two lads got off to a shaky start in training. Mike taught them how kindness would be of mutual benefit and slowly but surely barriers were broken down and a respect that at the start of their relationship seemed impossible blossomed between these two lads. It's a lesson for us all about the power of kindness.

Mike explained:

When I was drill instructor at Marine Corps Recruit Depot San Diego, we had this Mexican kid from Los

Angeles and a Caucasian kid from Wyoming, a mountain area in the States. Two very, very different environments. The Wyoming kid had never seen or interacted with a Hispanic man in his life before. Being honest, this was oil and water trying to mix. So, we had just finished a very hard-paced run and I gave the order for a shower and quick change of clothes. The Mexican kid accidentally bumped into the Wyoming recruit and it all kicked off. They're butt naked fighting in the shower and I had to run in with my squared away uniform and my Campaign Cover on to separate these two 6ft 1in. teenagers. When we eventually got them sorted, I took them for what we call 'Incentive Training' to get rid of all that negativity and then I made them bunk mates.

At this point they are as far away from being brothers in arms as you could imagine, but there is no escaping for any recruit the need to show respect and kindness to each other. Otherwise they won't have the mentality that we need on the battlefield, because the ultimate act of kindness is to be prepared to lay down your life for your brother. As bunk mates, these lads were now responsible for each other. They knew that if one failed in a task or slipped up, they would both have to pay the consequences.

After thirteen weeks of training, just before graduation into the Marines, we allow the families to come and see where the recruits have been trained and they are able to see every part of the barracks. During that day we designate guards to make sure nothing goes missing and I made the Mexican kid one of the guards because his parents could not afford to make the trip. But the Caucasian recruit requested to speak with me the night prior to family day and asked me to find another guard because he wanted his brother (the Mexican recruit) to spend the day with him and his family. You have to understand that during training the drill instructor is like a god to these men so that Wyoming Marine showed courage and proved his depth of kindness by coming to me that night. It was remarkable to see the transformation in their relationship – the teamwork, cohesion and the commitment to one another was complete. That's real kindness in action.

Mike's story about the Mexican and Wyoming lads shows how the power of kindness can be absolutely transformative, even when cultivated in the places you least expect it, and can lead to incredibly strong and valued relationships.

An act of kindness to someone who has offered the opposite to you can have a major impact. If you can maintain the moral high ground and be 'bigger' than the person being unkind, then that shows mental fortitude – and the chances are that the other person will in fact respond to this. It's not always easy to work out what to do if someone is being the opposite of kind, but a soft, caring response can often take the sting out of a barbed comment, and you'll often find that you feel much better too. Meeting unkindness with kindness derails anger, and all the ugly emotions and reactions that can bring, replacing it with understanding and empathy.

Kindness in leadership

One great example of why the Royal Marines has such a record of success is in the training of its leaders and, despite their tough exterior, kindness has to be part of those leaders' DNA. Inspirational leadership is important for any business or team, and a kind, compassionate leader who puts their people at the centre of everything is someone who is likely to improve that team, as well as generate the respect of the people that they have the privilege to lead. Leaders set the tone and environment, and I am convinced that those leaders who show genuine empathy and kindness will get the best out of their colleagues. Sadly, we all probably know of examples where inspirational leadership is lacking. Ego often gets in the way of being able to motivate and inspire, and you regularly see people at the top who believe the only way to lead is through fear. They may be in a high position, but I've seen many who aren't prepared to lead by example and who will always ask others to do the things they are not prepared to do themselves. That's not leadership, in my opinion.

It can be easy for work colleagues to become disheartened or simply go through the motions when they don't feel a sense of empathy from those in leadership roles. This is rare in the Marines, but I am well aware of how it impacts the business world. A strong leader, as I have experienced, will know who in their team has been pivotal behind any shared successes; they will know those who have grafted and put in the hard yards to make it happen. In turn, those team members know that they will be well rewarded for their efforts. It sounds simple, even obvious, and yet even such a small act of kindness as a 'well done' can often be lacking in the workplace. Believe me, a kind word of praise for someone's efforts will be returned ten-fold.

I have had the privilege to have worked alongside some truly inspirational leaders across military, sport and business, and the very greatest of those are kind and compassionate, setting the tone for how people behave with each other.

Kindness to oneself

One aspect of kindness that often goes unmentioned is the fact that being compassionate comes at a cost, because it requires an incredible amount of energy and effort. I know that feeling from my time as the CO of Hasler Company, as we sought to support our patients through their own journey of recovery and help them rebuild their lives.

For two years I was working six days a week, sometimes leaving the house at 4 a.m. to arrive at 5.30. During the work day I would engage in some physical training, and would support my team in giving their all for those under our care, pulling together the various strands of help to make sure each person had a clear plan to recovery – if that was possible. Sometimes your best just couldn't be enough because of the severity of the situation. That's hard to handle, and if you find yourself in that situation, I can relate. I know how hard it is. But you cannot beat yourself up, you must focus on the fact that you did everything you can, otherwise it is easy to slip to a dark place that will only be bad for you and those around you.

I've always been one of those who has been good at separating work from home life, which is a vital skill to learn, but I have to admit that the lines became blurred when I was Hasler Company CO. My wife Suzanne could see how it was affecting me: the burden of having these wounded warriors in my care was very heavy and being the top boss can be a very lonely place because there is only one of you. So, if you're at the very pinnacle of your business or profession and feeling lonely at times, then I fully understand. Watching people deteriorate in front of you is not pleasant and can make you feel very helpless. That was the toughest part and it brought home to me the important question of who cares for the carers? Who really cares about the leaders? We're all human and everyone, no matter how high their position, will need someone to talk to – and they too will need and appreciate that sympathetic ear and act of kindness from time to time.

To be kind to others, it is important to also be kind to yourself. To do so, you need to learn how to look inward and reflect on the impact your kindness has on your own state of mind. You need to learn to recognise when you need to replenish your stores, when you need to take some time to be kind to yourself, and put yourself first for a while. Because without doing so, you will wear yourself out and no longer be able to offer kindness to those around you. Kindness, like everything else, is a balancing act between giving and taking, and it demands that we take care of ourselves. Your voyage towards kindness should always start with you, and then emanate out toward others.

Don't let anyone tell you that kindness or showing your vulnerabilities is somehow a weakness. That only reveals their character and not yours. Being kind shows strength of character and high moral fibre.

Kindness is also contagious, so go out and spread some. Make people smile and know that regular and consistent acts of kindness are critical to living your life to its fullest.

CHAPTER 7: KINDNESS LESSON SUMMARY

Remember ...

* A small act of kindness can go a long way.
* Being kind to others creates a strong bond between people.
* The benefits of kindness include enhanced mental wellbeing and feelings of life fulfilment.

Step 1 – WHAT is kindness?

Kindness is the quality of being friendly, generous and considerate. It is being selfless, unconditionally caring and compassionate to other people on a consistent basis. Kindness is a trait that shows in your actions and words to others, which help others to feel good about themselves – but also have a hugely positive impact on you. Kindness is a positive trait and requires the giver to think of others before themselves.

Step 2 – WHY is kindness important?

A single of act of kindness can make your environment a happier place to inhabit, for everyone. It can boost feelings of confidence and engender belief in yourself and others. Being kind can foster positive changes from both a mental and a physical perspective, and it is linked to better health, mindfulness and an increased sense of self-worth in both the giver and the receiver.

Step 3 – HOW to become more kind in your life.

+ Firstly, be kind to yourself and allow it to emanate out to others.
+ If someone is kind to you, pass it on to others and watch it grow. Kindness is contagious.
+ Practise acts of kindness even when no one is watching; do not seek recognition for it.
+ When someone is unkind or even hateful, meet it with kindness; you will be amazed at the result.
+ Be kind every single day. Consider kindness before you speak or act, and observe your relationships grow and flourish.

CHAPTER 8

Humility

Definition: The quality of having a modest view of your own importance.

The tears were streaming down my face. I was presenting my great friend and colleague Paul 'Baz' Barrett with his medal at the Wounded Warriors Games in Camp Pendleton, near San Diego, California. Just a couple of years earlier Baz's life had been, quite literally, blown apart, but now he was being hailed by 2,000 newly acquired American fans as one of their heroes.

In 2008 Baz had been leading a troop of Royal Marines in Helmand Province, Afghanistan, where his men were right on the frontline of the ongoing battle against the Taliban. Baz is a quiet, outstanding Senior Mountain Leader with vast amounts of experience, who would put his head where others would fear to put their boot – and few in my experience have exuded humility more.

In Afghanistan at this time the fighting had moved from direct force-on-force kinetic engagements with rifles and bayonets to having to deal with counter-insurgency operations against IEDs that the Taliban had been laying down in their attempt to kill or injure our lads and to erode morale. The weeks of constant battle with the enemy was mentally draining and sadly many were being maimed or killed by these IEDs. Baz had seen too many of his young men suffer at the hands of these IEDs, so he decided that he would be the lead man in seeking to locate these hidden explosives. Demonstrating extreme courage, Baz led from the front as they crossed the explosive-riddled ground.

Baz knew that the odds were not in his favour when it came to the likelihood of him suffering at the hands of one of these explosives. It was an incredible act of humility by such a highly respected sergeant. But Baz understood that even though he was of higher rank than his lads, this did not mean that his life was any more valuable than those of his men. Humility is a way of behaving that shows that you don't think you are better or more important than other people. Performing an act of heroic service like this towards his men is indicative of Baz's humble nature, for which he is well known.

One day Baz knelt and triggered a hugely devastating roadside bomb. He was severely injured, one of his hands was eviscerated and he lost a leg, leaving him with a stump. He additionally suffered devastating head and torso injuries and would have died were it not for the quick thinking of his team, the advances in medical technology and the speed with which the Medical Extraction Response Team got him to a hospital.

It was a massive blow, Baz was universally acknowledged to be the best sergeant in the entire Unit and although he survived, he would have the unwanted record of any Armed Forces serviceman of undergoing the highest number of operations after being injured in action: fifty-seven to date. Stepping up in the way that Baz did, putting his life on the line because he considered it of no greater importance than those of his brothers by his side, is a tremendous act of humility and courage, and one we can all be challenged by and learn from. He has gone down in Royal Marines history as a true legend and someone that I greatly respect.

This is how Baz recalls the moment that changed his life forever:

I wouldn't be here today if it wasn't for the quick actions of those around me when I stepped on that IED. The sergeant major recalls moments immediately after the explosion – how I was trying to patch myself back together. My right leg had landed 60 metres from the IED. He also recalled that as he took me away in the jeep I turned around and asked him why he was driving like a maniac. He just laughed at me. My life was hanging in the balance, I was given 52 litres of blood and I actually died at one point in the helicopter and (on my way) back to the UK.

People talk about heroes and legends but I've never thought of myself as a hero. Heroes are very special people. Being a Marine meant being in combat; that was what I signed up for. I was doing my job and that's the biggest compliment I could have been given.

Sometimes humility costs. Being humble and putting others first almost cost Baz his life. But it was that same humility that allowed him to accept how his life had changed and then embrace new challenges. Now, standing on the podium receiving his medal, he was still humble, crediting the inspiration of those around him. 'When I got to the Wounded Warrior Games, I was inspired by those around me. Whether it was a mental or physical disability, they gave their all. I had to humbly accept that I couldn't do the things I did before, but I could do new things, different things and that was crucial for me.'

Being humble doesn't mean not striving to achieve incredible things – Baz's story is testimony to that! It is about the way in which you strive: not treading on the toes of others but putting others first; not seeing yourself as the most important but valuing everyone equally; not expecting praise or reward but doing your job with pride.

Understated excellence

We always talk about understated excellence in the Marines. We expect it from our people. We let our excellence speak for itself rather than shouting from the rooftops about what we do and how good we are. We never describe the Marines as 'elite', and instead leave that to others to decide. Humility runs throughout all our successes and it's a value that can have such a powerful impact on any collective body. Being under-stated is a strength. It's not about being quiet, or shying away from challenges; it's more about that ego-less self-assurance that comes with a life dedicated to building high levels of self-discipline, self-confidence and self-belief. It takes drive, commitment and dedication to get to that point where you can link being understated to being excellent in a modest way that exudes professional quality in all that you do. People will notice the change in you if you can maintain your humility while striving for excellence – a quality which is discussed more in Chapter 12.

As we saw in Baz's story, it is possible to strive for excel-lence while being humble. Contrary to what some may think, humility and a competitive nature can exist alongside each other. I know this because Marines are some of the most competitive people you are ever likely to meet. We don't overtly compete with our peers, but we do compete with ourselves and the 'standard'. That standard has been set and is maintained over many years and seeking to exceed that standard is built into our ethos, but not at the cost of being unkind to someone else, or by selling somebody short just to make yourself look good. You can be competitive in the right way. It is all about the mindset – focusing on being the best you can be, rather than on beating others. One thing I have noticed since leaving the Royal Marines and entering civilian life is the manner in which many people are overtly competitive against each other for promotion or whatever they are seeking to get out of their job. In the Marines, there is an understanding that doing the best you can do without crapping on other people is the way to be. Follow this, and you will get that promotion when you earn it – and not by beating someone else. We all hate to lose, but we don't have to sacrifice humility to be some of the most driven and ambitious people on the planet. In fact, humility is a part of this drive. In combat, there is no time to stop and admire yourself and the work you're engaging in, because the mission comes first.

The danger of arrogance

The danger of striving for – and achieving – excellence is, of course, arrogance. This is the opposite of humility and can be the downfall of an individual, a company, a school, even a government. The main danger of arrogance is that it obscures rational judgement, often causing people to make poor decisions through a lack of self-awareness. Being dangerously over-confident or arrogant doesn't sit well with me. In fact, on many occasions, I have seen it lead to complacency and reduced levels of performance. And being arrogant is not a healthy or happy way to live; living in a state of arrogance can lead to a world where you live in constant fear of failure or of being humiliated. It will be no surprise for you to hear that arrogant people are not popular, either, and others tend to avoid them at every opportunity. A humble person is more socially orientated than self-centred, is honest with themselves and values feed-back from others. A humble person is absent of any bias; they don't favour one over another and are prepared to show their vulnerabilities and embrace failure. Be grateful for what you have and above all don't spend your time being boastful and telling everyone how great you are. No one likes a show-off, after all.

Royal Marines quietly get on with things without bragging. They recognise the flaws in their own character, they humbly see the defects they have to deal with, and that doesn't leave any room for complacency or arrogance. It also means that we are always learning and always improving, because we are open to feedback, and this actually means we achieve more than we would if we believed ourselves to already be perfect.

This is the Marine way, but it is something that new recruits often have to learn. We get a lot of young men who arrive with good fitness levels and maybe a bit of confidence or even arrogance because they might have a black belt in karate or an Olympic medal, for example. What I've found is that these types of people are often not open to personal growth. Arrogant recruits think they already know it all and therefore have nothing further to learn – the reality is that they either learn humility, and fast, or they drop out. For those who can learn the art of humility, with this comes a new element of teachability, and that allows a person to be open to new ideas and improvements, which can lead them to new levels of performance that they never thought possible. Humility is an important stepping stone to success.

There have been times when we have seen a glimpse of arrogance on display at the end of certain activities, such as someone celebrating their success and belittling others for their lack of achievement in a task. That is stamped out very quickly. It is the polar opposite of what we demand in the

Marines and is simply not allowed to develop and fester. We have no room for arrogance because it is the enemy of success.

During Marines training, if you show any evidence of your own self-importance then you are marked down on what is called Personal Qualities (PQs). At the end of every week of training, the section corporal will record your scores in various tests, and there will also be comments on your PQs. The recruit will have the opportunity to read each weekly report to receive the honest and open feedback he needs. This is where the corporal makes it clear exactly what is expected of him. By its nature, this level of accountability encourages a humble attitude in every recruit. Put simply, you can ace all the tests, but if you don't have the personal values expected of a Royal Marine, the green beret will not be for you.

While humility can be so empowering in the individual's life, it also breeds unity in a team, especially when all the members share a sense of purpose that brings them together. Great teams form a ring of steel that nothing can penetrate and it starts with being humble. Much like the All Blacks, arguably the greatest team in sporting history, whose well-documented sense of belonging always starts with players being humble enough to 'sweep the sheds'. It's a term from the All Blacks' ritual of players grabbing a broom and sweeping out the dressing room after a game. Even the most celebrated of players are prepared to pick up a brush and clean up their own mess. This type of selfless attitude brings the team together, reminding them that they are all responsible for the wellbeing of the team, that no one is above doing the small or dirty jobs. It establishes equality, a high level of trust and forms deep bonds in any team. It helps to drive a culture of team spirit and togetherness. There are similar parallels with the Royal Marines, who place humility at the top of its values, because we know that from this one value we can go on to build respect, loyalty, a sense of belonging and high performance within our people.

Humility in leadership

Humility is just as important – or even more so – in a leader. It is sometimes said that someone in a leadership position should be forced to eat some 'humble pie' every so often. Personally I think it should be on the breakfast table every morning.

Great leaders will give their team more of the credit when things go well and take more of the responsibility when things don't. But we don't always see this. Many leaders will come up short if humility is in short supply. It is important to realising that in any position, however high and powerful, we need other people, we cannot do it alone. Once you recognise this truth, you will automatically show humility, gratitude and respect towards those on your team. I am thankful to have had many role models of humility in positions of leadership during my time in the Marines. Baz was one – his decision to lead from the front showed great humility in that he did not value his life, as a commander, any higher than the lives of his troops. He recognised that his rank conferred responsibility, it did not signify greater individual worth.

This was demonstrated in a more light-hearted but equally telling way on the day when the Corps Regiment Sergeant Major, the Commandant General's right-hand man and the highest ranking non-commissioned officer, came to the Physical Training Instructor's staff room. That room had a certain code of conduct based around humour. So, for example, when you were on a break and there were twelve or more in the room, it was a rule that anyone could shout 'Dice' and that meant that the person who rolled the lowest score had to go into the 'Tank', a stagnant 6-foot-deep pool of water designed to catch Marines falling from a rope above a chasm on the assault course that the men had to crawl across. If a double-one was rolled then everybody had to go in – no exceptions! The Corps RSM, being a PTI himself, was more than aware of this rule, so before entering the room he took a swift glance left and then right, did a quick headcount and, believing it was all clear, popped inside for a cup of tea. To his astonishment, a load of us jumped out from inside the lockers. There were now more than twelve in the room and up went the cry of 'Dice!'

At this point he was in full blues uniform with medals and regalia, and was just twenty minutes away from being on parade with the general to inspect and pass out the new batch of officers as one of the VIPs, an important once-per-year event. He breathed a sigh of relief when he rolled an eleven, but then on the last roll of the dice up came the two single digits. The cry of 'snake eyes!' almost took the roof off. As Royal Marines PTIs, we have a saying that 'nobody is bigger than the branch'. The Corps RSM made a telephone call over to the Officers' Mess. 'Commandant General Sir, I'm not going to the parade, I'm going in the tank instead.' So there he was, hanging from the rope, twenty feet up, before doing a backwards somersault into the static tank in his full blues uniform, medals and all! It reminded us all that humility sticks with you, no matter how far you go up the ranks. It wasn't even up for discussion because the RSM knew that he would be breaking the code of humility that belonged not only to the PTI Branch but throughout every aspect of the Royal Marines. I was a young NCO at the time, but it made me respect the RSM all the more, and the memory has stayed with me.

Cultivating humility

By being humble you will become more satisfied in life and it will improve your relationships with others. It will help open you up to fuller, richer experiences. If you think you know it all, then you won't be open-minded enough to seek out new things to learn and you will stagnate. This is linked to a fixed mindset and is the opposite of the growth mindset that we seek to adopt to optimise our personal and professional development.

Humility, just like the other values discussed in this book, can be learned. Start by looking within at yourself, recognising any weaknesses and admitting to yourself that you're not the best at everything. No matter how gifted you might be, there is always room for improvement. Only after looking at yourself can you look at others, removing any preconceived judgments you may have. Judging others only leads to troubled relationships, so clear your mind and become open to positive change and making incremental developments. Everybody makes mistakes – even you. When people fail at something, the natural reaction is to find something or someone else to blame, but if you want to be humble, then the first thing you will look at is yourself. By doing this, you take personal responsibility of the situation; you take owner-ship of your own mistakes by eliminating any excuses, which means you can then use them as an opportunity to grow. If you aren't humble enough to recognise it in the first place, you'll never be able to improve upon it.

To become more humble, avoid bragging or talking down to people, especially those in your charge, your peers, and particularly youngsters and others who are less experienced and might look to you for inspiration. Equally, when things go well, humble people see the importance of giving others credit. In fact, they often naturally deflect attention away from themselves. Brash and loud people tend to be hiding behind something, often their own inadequacies – either a lack of knowledge, experience or confidence. We all know someone like this. Learn to recognise it, as it usually all comes out in the wash anyway.

CHAPTER 8: HUMILITY LESSON SUMMARY

Remember ...

- ◆ Don't ask anyone to do something that you wouldn't.
- ◆ Keep your feet on the ground – it will serve you well.
- ◆ Humble people who are genuinely open to feedback often overtake their more naturally talented peers.

Step 1 – WHAT is humility?

Humility is the quality of having a modest view of your own importance. Humility relates to the extent to which we place our own personal interests above others.

Step 2 – WHY is humility important?

Humility has a powerful impact on people because it directly relates to your strength of character. Humility connects with our ability to assimilate information and, as such, humble people are better learners and problem solvers. Humble people are excellent at building rapport with others and tend to form stronger, deeper relationships.

Step 3 – HOW to be more humble in your life.

- Leave ego at the door.
- Compete with yourself, not with others.
- Be thankful but never boastful.
- Be open to positive change; listen to others and take their advice on board.
- Show your vulnerable side; people will notice the change in you

CHAPTER 9

Understanding

Definition: Having clarity and knowledge about someone or a situation.

Under the cover of darkness, somebody was in our small amphibious assault speedboat who shouldn't have been. Our section corporal was supposed to have counted in seven men, but there were eight sitting in full battle uniform and camouflage cream. The corporal quickly pulled out his torch to see what was going on and then came to one man sitting beside me who he didn't recognise. 'Hey,' he said, 'you're not one of my men. You shouldn't be here.' To which came the reply: 'You're right, sir. I'm the Duke of Edinburgh, but today I'm one of your men.'

For sixty-four years, HRH Prince Philip, The Duke of Edinburgh was the Captain General of the Royal Marines, and having had the privilege of meeting him on several occasions, I know for a fact he was particularly proud of that role. The Marines are a family, but you don't have to wear a green beret to be part of it – and that goes from the Queen right down to the newest recruit.

That first encounter I had with Prince Philip was just after I had earned my green beret in 1988, and it was great to see just how much the Marines meant to him. His military knowledge was incredible, as were his strict standards; if you happened to have a button out of place on your uniform, he would notice. He also spoke our language; in the Marines we have our own words for things, such as a 'scran' for food or 'dhobi' for washing. The Duke mucked in with everyone else as we carried out our training, tagging alongside the corporal, and we had a great time with him. He loved spending time with 'his' Marines.

The Duke understood us and we understood him because he was one of us. Understanding those around you means you have to invest time, energy and emotion in those people, and it is never wasted. Indeed, it can help resolve problems more quickly, before they escalate from a flickering flame to an inferno of conflict, whether that be in a marriage, a family scenario, a sports team or a business. Genuine and authentic engagement lends itself to having a thorough understanding of the world around you and it allows you to have a positive impact that can be so rewarding for all concerned.

Marines care and want the best for each other, so we take that extra time to get alongside mates or, in the case of a good leader, to be aware of how your men are developing and feeling about life as a Royal Marine. Investing in the people around you reaps high dividends.

Understanding yourself

The first step toward strengthening understanding is to recognise your own traits and be honest about your own strengths and weaknesses. By doing this, you will be able to see how you tend to act. Are you an introvert or extrovert? Are you spontaneous, pragmatic or idealistic? By identifying your own character type, you will become more aware of how you act in certain situations based on your personality. This will then allow you to make minor adjustments based on the traits you want to try to change or tweak. You can't change who you are, but you *can* change how you act.

Maybe it's the case that you need to pause to understand and be honest with yourself as you consider your own approach to people and life in general – to try to see how you impact people, for good or otherwise. I think it is important to have that moment, to have a little time for self-reflection.

Taking the time to understand yourself also impacts on how you understand others. You can apply the same observations to others to help you understand where they are coming from. Again, it's not about judging others or trying to get them to think like you, but about identifying certain traits in others so you can better understand their perspectives.

During my time in the Royal Marines, I witnessed how

the Corps has developed and learned to understand people in a better way so that each individual can grow and become even better members of this special team. It's about continuous improvement. Understanding what lies behind the reaction, or possibly the lack of a response, from someone can be so beneficial. Before leaping to conclusions about why someone has responded in that way, you must try to read the situation and understand what is going on. Why might that person have acted in that particular way? Perhaps they are having a difficult time with a certain situation or it holds certain triggers for them. It could just be that they hold a different set of central beliefs to you and see life through a different prism.

Once you've taken the time and effort to understand and get to know someone, it also becomes much easier to spot when they are behaving out of character. On many occasions I have witnessed this springing from peer pressure. For example, in a group situation, someone may not feel comfortable giving the answer they know to be true, so they clam up. To the teacher or the leader, that can come across as an attitude of disengagement, but with a little more effort of understanding, you can get to the core of the issue and unlock someone's potential. We often see it in young people in communities, when their peers have them shackled to certain ways of behaviour. It's a burden that needs to be thrown off, and an understanding leader can help show them a path to escape this peer pressure.

Embracing difference

A little understanding really can go a long way, and that's why I've found it so important to do my best not to pre-judge anyone. It is something I have learnt to do better over the years, because earlier in life I would have been guilty of judging a book by its cover. Hopefully, however, as I've got older, I've become a little wiser.

Once you understand that people are not always what they may seem, or are not what others say they are, you real-ise that maybe they just need some understanding of their background or a second chance. After all, we all make mis-takes and sometimes conclusions can be made through false assumptions. So, the first step to understanding is to let go of judgement or any pre-conceived ideas you may have based on how someone looks, their background, gender, character, hair colour or customs. One of our greatest strengths should be that our world is full of unique and diverse people, yet we often don't take the time to truly understand those who are different to us.

Accepting our differences and recognising alternate points of view is a good way learn to listen to and understand others. Labelling people is unhelpful, and often leads to making a decision based on incomplete or even wrong information. It also opens the door to confirmation bias. This means that once you have labelled someone, you will start to interpret all their actions through the lens of that label in order to fit with the view you already have of them. So if you label someone as 'difficult', if they raise an alternative opinion you might immediately see this as an example of them being antagonistic or contrary, whereas in fact they are simply proposing an alternative – and potentially better – idea. Confirmation bias is a dangerous habit to fall into, because we tend to be blind to the fact that we are doing it. Recognising it in yourself is the first step to defeating it. So try to have an open mind and seek to truly understand where a person is coming from with no previous bias.

Because we are all different, we naturally have different strengths and weaknesses, so it's also about maximising those different skillsets and adding breadth to a community or a team. It is important to be willing to understand that someone may need more help in a certain area than others to get through a problem or situation – and vice-versa, someone close might have the necessary skills or expertise that can assist in a certain area.

Mental health

We have already encountered the Marines saying: 'Be first to understand, the first to adapt and respond, and the first to overcome.'

Like many other organisations and employers, the Marines have had to do a lot of work in recent years around how they approach mental health struggles. One of the first things that we had to confront as an institution was that having an issue with mental health could be automatically perceived as a sign of weakness and, as a result, that it could affect someone's career and their progress up the Marines ladder. We recognised this and made inroads to change this perception and the stigma surrounding mental health. This work is ongoing, as any process of understanding should be. It was something that I had to learn as a young Marine and was still learning as commander of Hasler Company, which was formed in 2006 to rehabilitate and help to remove the stigma attached to those who had suffered physical and/or mental injuries.

In the Marines we found that advocating a proactive attitude towards mental health was far more effective than a reactive approach. We had to encourage people to engage with their mental health on a daily basis in the same way as they did with their physical health. In this way people were more likely to have an understanding of what good mental health looked like and recognise when they themselves or others around them were suffering. We realised that people were more likely to come forward with mental health concerns if there was easy access for them to do so, but only if it could be accessed without the involvement or knowledge of their peers or managers and if total confidentially was assured. This led to a gradual change in the perception and understanding surrounding mental health issues. Cultural change takes time, however, and only by putting in place practices that drive and endorse effective treatment will the cultural shift take hold.

It's the same in wider society: once people have summoned up the nerve to seek mental health support, they must then have direct and immediate access to it. Individuals, and sometimes families, often carry the burden of mental health issues alone and only seek professional mental health care when a problem is already out of control. Sometimes the response is too late. We must all realise that our mental health is as important as our physical health. Just as if you had a physical injury, you would go to a doctor to get a diagnosis and subsequent treatment, seeking mental health treatment should become an accepted part of our everyday lives.

My first experience in the Marines of someone suffering with their mental health came very early on in my career, during my first deployment, which was in Belfast. Right from the moment we arrived we had to face weekly mass riots, blast bombs and shootings in north Belfast. At times I was apprehensive, but then I got used to it. However, I knew it was becoming too much for some, who were struggling to come to terms with the pressures of modern-day operations.

This was during the 1980s, when an admission of mental health issues was often perceived as a weakness. It was never discussed; you were expected to just push through regardless of the fallout. I watched people break and crumble under extreme stress and pressure. It is not nice to see. We have come a long way since then, in conversation, in attitude, in the improved access to support. There is still a long way to go, however.

Understanding while holding conflicting beliefs

The act of understanding is not plain sailing – in fact it can be extremely difficult. This is particularly evident when you get a conflict of beliefs or morals. Seeing another point of view can be challenging at times, especially when it's the polar opposite of what you believe. Only by taking the time to listen to and understand someone else's viewpoint will you be able to see their perspective and respect their personal beliefs, even if you do not personally agree. The important thing to remember is that this is OK. You don't have to agree with everyone – in fact, it would be a very boring world if we did! But you can disagree in a way that is respectful, and key to this is ensuring that you have taken the time to understand their perspective – with an open mind – and treat it seriously. Hopefully they will then offer you the same courtesy.

When two perspectives simply will not align, then there is the potential for conflict. We see it time and time again. But through understanding – not necessarily agreeing! – you can defuse that conflict and find a rational, neutral way forward. You don't grow by arguing or entering into conflict with other people; you grow by gaining new insights, ideas and perspectives. Find middle ground if you can, but if not, then calmly explain your perspective and peacefully disagree. Try to get away from aggressively dominating another person with your opinion by encouraging discussion not hostility, which can diffuse the potential for the escalation of arguments and confrontation.

Understanding the importance of diversity and genuinely taking on board that other people have different ways at looking at things that are not necessarily right or wrong is crucial. Everyone has their own unique set of life experiences that prompt them to think and perceive things in a certain way. The right mix of differing values and unique perspectives adds to the team dynamic and helps a team or organisation go to another level. Even within the family, where you might assume everyone is coming from a similar background or mindset, remember that each individual also has other, separate experiences outside the family unit that they might hold differing opinions, and remember to respect that individuality. Different ideas and beliefs should enhance society rather than be used to bring division. You can understand without necessarily agreeing, but only if you are prepared to listen to each other in a non-confrontational and respectful way.

Understanding in society

I really believe we need a society that is prepared to do the hard yards of understanding, to understand difference and value it – realising that someone will bring something to that life situation that you don't and vice versa.

The same can be said of your family situation, or maybe your workplace. Do your colleagues know you are comfortable and willing to sit down and genuinely listen to their perspective? Do kids at school feel at ease with approaching a teacher to unburden themselves? Can you get beyond your own personality and understand the issue, big or small, through the eyes of someone else?

The willingness to understand yourself and others better will require you to adopt a perpetual growth mindset where you embark on a never-ending journey of self-awareness, self-reflection and self-improvement. It is important that we continue to actively cultivate understanding throughout life, no matter your age or position, so that we can continue to contribute to the world around us. As the Greek philosopher Socrates rightly put it, 'An unexamined life is not worth living.'

Understanding should be an active part of your life. Not

something you only draw upon when it is needed, but something you actively set out to do. This requires time and conscious effort. It is often useful to step back and make that time to understand the people around you, the environment and the situation before you can assess what they might need, and how you might be able to provide that. So stop, take a look around and consider where you are as a person, as a business, a club or a family. Does something need to change? Do you truly understand the needs of those around you?

By making the time to understand ourselves and others, we can build better connections with people. If we can inspire each other to contribute positively then the community, school, workplace or sports team is better for it. We can learn from each other, celebrate our differences and build a sense of unity and belonging based on selflessness. When you build connected relationships in this way, you can enjoy sharing the special moments together and you can create an environment where you feel comfortable in sharing your issues, your hopes, dreams and fears with those people who care about you by your side. By standing tall next to each other, we get through the dark times and walk into the light – together.

CHAPTER 9: UNDERSTANDING
LESSON SUMMARY

Remember ...

♦ The first step towards understanding is to let go of judgement.
♦ To understand others, you first need to understand yourself.
♦ Your understanding has to constantly evolve as situations change.

Step 1 – WHAT is understanding?

Understanding is having clarity and knowledge about a person or a situation. Understanding requires you to actively listen to others, to offer an empathetic ear and to develop good insight and judgement towards the feelings of others.

Step 2 – WHY is understanding important?

Relationships are stronger when rooted in understanding. Understanding builds bridges between people, improving collaboration and cooperation, and helping avoid conflict or anger. When time is taken to actively understand people and situations, then that information is held in the memory for much longer. This aids us in understanding different viewpoints, attitudes and experiences, and helps us to identify with people who may look at life through a different prism. Understanding also allows us to better grasp changing situations and therefore adapt and make the most of them.

Step 3 – HOW to be more understanding in your life?

- Understand yourself first and be honest about your own strengths and weaknesses.
- Take the time to understand other people's perspectives, especially those who differ from your own.
- Don't pre-judge – a little understanding can go a long way.
- Be an active listener – this means giving someone your entire attention and pausing to reflect on what they say.
- Take a proactive approach to recognising the state of your own mental health and that of others around you.

CHAPTER 10

Cheerfulness

Definition: A persona characterised by being happy and positive.

All gardeners know what a pain it is to have to deal with an overgrown garden. But just imagine if that grass was inside your front room. That's what faced one of the lads in 1991 when he returned to his house after fighting in the Gulf War and struggled to get the door open because there was eighteen inches of the stuff growing in there. While he'd been gone, we had sown it into his carpet and watered it every day for the length of time he had been in the Middle East. After finally getting the door open, he fetched a lawn mower and started cutting the grass in his front room! That's Marines humour for you.

Cheerfulness and good humour may not quickly come to

mind when you're thinking about the efficiency of a fighting unit like the Marines, but believe me it's critical. It is a key value that's looked for in those going through training because Marines know how important it is when you find yourself in a tough spot. A strong sense of humour helps us come to terms with the real dangers we face. This is also true of the many trials and tribulations you might face in civilian life; when you're under the cosh, humour can be a key element to bouncing back. It's a pressure release, but also a building block for unity and friendship because you laugh 'with' people, not 'at' them. The best friendships always contain some laughter. Humour can even help regulate a relationship that might otherwise struggle with competitiveness or other difficult emotions. That's how it was between me and former Royal Marines Major Molly McPherson, a Special Forces Mountain Leader and all-round Marines legend. PTIs and Mountain Leaders have a strong rivalry that is borne from respect for each other, but that rivalry often spills into lots of good-humoured one-upmanship.

Molly and I did a Norway deployment together, both as leaders, and the wind-ups were constant. For a laugh, he super-glued my training shoes to the floor, but I got my own back when he was leaving for home and made the mistake of leaving his kit outside the door in preparation for heading to the airport. I got my skis on and shot halfway up the mountain, grabbed an 18lb boulder and packed it at the bottom of his Bergen rucksack. It was only when he got to Oslo airport and had to pay £200 for excess baggage that he realised there was an extra little 'Scotty' present in his kit!

Molly got the last laugh, however, at the tail end of a

dinner in Poole one night. After a few beers, I was snooz-ing on a sofa in the hallway with my mouth open, snoring away (a rooky error!). I could have been catching flies, but instead Molly was feeding me dead, blackened skin from the sole of his foot which had suffered frost bite due to his latest Antarctic expedition. I can still taste it now . . .

Now, I'm not saying that you feed anyone dead skin – I fully accept that Marines humour can be a bit much for some people! – but developing a sense of mutual humour with those around you can be such a help in life because we all need joy in our lives.

Cheerfulness might seem small, or less important, in com-parison to some of the other values we have looked at, but you should not underestimate the power of cheerfulness. In adversity, it can bring you strength, resilience and fortitude. It can enable you to pick yourself up and continue when the chips are down. It can help you see the silver lining. In hap-pier times, it can help you recognise what you have and be grateful for it. It makes a person a joy to be around.

The benefits of cheerfulness

Cheerfulness in the face of adversity is considered an essential requirement for a Marine and those carrying out the green beret training are seeking to identify this critical value during the thirty-two weeks of high-intensity training. The way the Marines view it, if you can't see the lighter side in training, then when the real pressure is at its greatest, you might not be able to cope. I passed that test one lovely evening, skiing up a mountain in Norway. At twilight things don't quite look the same and I remember seeing this Marine flash past me, and then another and another. It turned out they weren't going past me; I was going past them – backwards. The light had tricked my eyes, and I was sliding backwards on my skis without knowing it. It only really dawned on me when I ended up hitting a tree; a common way for Marines to 'stop' in the Arctic! I could have been demoralised to find myself back where I started. I could have been embarrassed – my whole unit had just seen me slide backwards into a tree! But where would the fun have been in getting in a bad mood about it? Instead, I had a little giggle at myself and cracked on up the mountain.

All of us in life will have to handle difficult or awkward or pressurised situations, possibly caused by our own mistakes or maybe those of others, but a sense of humour is a great tool to help you make it through. Crucially, it can help you avoid escalating situations by choosing cheerfulness over losing your temper – or 'flashing' as we call it in the Marines. I know some people are more easily disposed to lose their temper than others, while others have a naturally cheerful and sunshiney disposition but, as with everything, the Marines believe that this is something that can be learned. My good friend Dan O'Mahoney actually trained himself to wake up with a smile if ever he was awakened in the middle of the night for sentry duty, when his natural reaction would be to react in a grumpy manner. After all, nobody likes being woken from a good sleep. It simply became a matter of habit – the minute he was woken, he would slap a grin on his face and it immediately made him feel better. Try it!

There is, however, a difference between encouraging your-self to see the lighter side and pretending. Not all of us are going to be Mr or Mrs Happy all the time, and trying to be can often lead to putting on a false face that will ultimately crack in the heat of family or work problems. Allow yourself to feel the first emotion that rises up in a situation, but then take a step back and actively consider if you can see a lighter side. If not, then that's fine. But if you can, why not let that lead your emotions instead? It's always worth a try.

Being able to see something funny in the toughest of times can be such a release of tension. It's a way of clearing your head so you can calmly see a way forward. Negative thoughts can be stressful and harmful; seeing the lighter side, finding a moment of humour, is an incredibly powerful way of elim-inating such thoughts and immediately reducing the stress. This allows you to re-set, re-focus and go again. By starting the process afresh, you can re-focus on what you're doing and replace the darker thoughts with a more optimistic outlook. Cheerfulness in adversity is about having that little wry smile, 'cracking a funny' and moving on.

This is a useful technique that I know is employed at the top level of sport in pressure moments, such as taking a penalty. At such times, being able to ease the tension, recon-nect, recover perspective and focus is something Marines do instinctively. We always try to find some humour in those difficult moments, using laughter to build hope and break the ice. Being able to have a giggle, or even just a small smile, also has physiological benefits, such as a release of dopamine, serotonin and other 'feel good' hormones that help to reduce stress. It even boosts your immunity! No matter whether at work or in a family setting, if you can find a way to release that tension and have a laugh together, the situation will almost certainly improve.

My fellow former Commando and great friend Dr Lara Herbert makes it clear why cheerfulness can be so powerful in the midst of some of the worst situations that you may encounter:

I carry a little card with all the Commando values written on it everywhere I go. I recently took this card on a six-month medical fellowship to Uganda, where I referred to it a few times. I worked in very busy tertiary referral hospital where the quantity of patients and the severity of their injuries and illnesses shocked me. It was relentless. The operating lists and queues never seemed to shorten. Resources were thin on the ground. Doctors often had to make extremely difficult triage decisions. Nursing capacity was stretched to unthinkable limits on a daily basis. And yet, what struck me the most was the smiles. Despite the fatigue, the stress, the complexity of their decisions and their insurmountable workloads, my Ugandan colleagues kept smiling and telling jokes. Their upbeat attitude most definitely buoyed me along and helped me through some seemingly impossible days. It was wonderful to see Commando values being demonstrated in this setting.

In a team situation when morale is low and things are tough, it often takes just one person to radiate cheerfulness and to lift all the other team members to a higher level of performance. That cheerfulness enables others to just keep going.

As Lara points out, cheerfulness is infectious – in a good way! So why not be that one person who brings a smile to the situation? And before you know it everyone will be feeling happier.

Cheerfulness in adversity

As Laura described so poignantly in the Ugandan hospital she worked in, cheerfulness is important to team dynamics. We have said that laughter is infectious and that it helps to remove tension, but it can also help to counter other non-productive emotions, such as doubt or fear. This was clearly demonstrated by my friend, the inspirational Mark Ormrod, when he stepped on an IED and lost both legs and an arm. As the medic rushed over to administer first aid, some of his first words were 'I think that's my disco dancing days over.' Mark knew his situation was bad, and I'm sure the fear could have been overwhelming for him. But instead of giving in to that fear – which could have had serious medical implications for him, such as increased blood loss – he reached for comedy. In this way, it can be a helpline in the darkest of moments.

A less life-threatening but still pretty sticky moment came to one of our four-man team, former Marine Andy Marcel, when patrolling in County Fermanagh one day. Due to the threat of the IRA, we had to make sure that we didn't get caught in obvious choke positions that would leave us stationary and therefore vulnerable to attack. So, instead of using gates, we would hop hedges and fences as we moved through fields and we became quite adept at it. That was fine until this particular wintry day when we landed in a field with what I can only describe as a super-bull in it – and he wasn't too happy to see anybody else in his territory. In this instance, it was every man for himself as we sprinted for safety beyond the next fence. Andy was last to go and, unfortunately, as he jumped, he landed right in the middle of the fence, legs apart on top of rusty barbed wire that tore his scrotum apart from top to bottom.

As I 'held him together' to stop the bleeding and waited for the helicopter to arrive for an emergency evacuation we all couldn't resist a little wry smile, knowing that Andy was never going to live this down. Every time we meet, I remind him that I kept his manhood intact!

Neither Andy nor Mark had much control over their situations, but sometimes you may be in a situation when you have brought the adversity upon yourself. In that case, a little humour, mixed with a lot of humility, will help you through. There's nothing like humour to salve a bit of wounded pride when you know you've messed up – it's an easy way to get through the situation without anyone thinking any less of you. If you sulk or complain or try to dodge the blame, people will not take well to this. But if you can hold your hands up and have a little laugh at yourself, people will soon be laughing with you and everyone moves on.

I had no option but to find some humour after one particular smelly experience during training in Norway. When you're operating in such extreme cold conditions, it is essential to fill your body with a lot of calories, so there is a lot of eating and drinking, and that of course means you have to go to the toilet quite often. When operating out in the sub-zero

Arctic conditions, we have specially made toilets called 'card-board crappers' with plastic bags inside, and everybody has to use these, no excuses, so as not to leave any trace that could be picked up by the enemy. Those full and pungent bags then have to be taken when we leave, so the waste of 150 Marines would be taken back by the logistical guys to an industrial facility where it could be disposed of. It was not a process I was aware of until I stepped out of line.

One weekend, a group of about ten of us were sitting drinking in the early hours of the morning after a week's hard graft in the mountains, and a few of us mentioned how hungry we were. We were miles from anywhere, in the Arctic wastelands; there was no local snack shop! I piped up and said I knew were to lay my hands on a big juicy turkey. I crawled past the guard and into the kitchen to grab the big bird which was immediately set on and instantly stripped bare by ten ravenously hungry Marines. Of course, the next day the boys' Sunday lunch was missing one of its three turkeys, and the sergeant major and colour sergeant demanded to know who the culprit was. I owned up – and paid the price. As punishment, instead of enjoying a long weekend skiing trip to the delights of Lillehammer, I was sent to the industrial facility where it was my job to melt the frozen crap of 150 Marines from the week and shove it down the plug hole of this massive bath. I'm not sure how cheerful I was at the time, but I got through it and learned a lesson. One minute you're top of the world, the next you're shovelling crap, so you'd better have a sense of humour.

We've all been through some tough, chaotic and even dark times in recent years and being able to stand back and find humour really does work to release tension and help you walk through that valley.

Cheerfulness in grief

A sense of cheerfulness is not always easy to find, and that's just a fact of life. The loss of a loved one, a friend, a colleague – or, in the case of the Marines, a brother or sister – will never be taken lightly, and for everyone facing such a moment the grieving process is unique. There is no blueprint that fits all who grieve. For me, and for many others I know, there is still, I believe, cheerfulness to be found to help us handle that loss. I know because I have lost many close brothers and sisters over the years and each has left their own mark on me and others around me. So, how do you find the cheerfulness within the grief? You get out the old photos, recall stories with fellow friends and family, and, critically, you mark each passing moment and remind yourself of the unique relation-ship you had with that person. You may even find yourselves laughing as you relive precious moments you shared with your loved one. Those memories are golden drops of joy etched in the memory and they can never be erased.

When we lose a brother or sister, there is often what we describe as a 'kit sale' – an unofficial event where about 100 guys from the deceased's company will come together for a sale of his personal stuff, which can range from a sock to a favourite t-shirt or even his green beret. I'm sure this may sound quite morbid to some, but there are two crucial points to this. First of all, it's a time to honour our fallen brother or sister, and we do it by sharing stories and having a drink and a laugh, just as we would have done with them when they were alive. Secondly, the sale raises thousands of pounds for their family. For example, a pair of shorts worth £7 can go for £1,500. Often mementoes are hung in the Company lines as a constant reminder for others yet to come that they will never be forgotten; one fallen hero had his ski pole bought and then framed with his name and rank underneath.

The pain of losing a comrade never lessens, but an event like this helps everyone because we feel we have paid our respects in the way a Marine would appreciate – and it also has a practical impact. It is an opportunity to truly honour our fallen brothers, which is not possible when in the middle of a mission. They are not usually sombre events, they are filled with conversation, reminiscing, companionship. Often the dark humour that is always around the Marines environment comes out in these moments, and the humour is cathartic, even if it is only for a few hours.

Cheerfulness and leadership

The Marines do not train us to handle every situation in a monastic, serious manner, but instead sow the seeds for a culture of operating with cheerfulness when the pressure is at its highest. They often inject humour into some pretty sketchy training conditions. So, for example, when in icy sub-zero conditions of -30, going through a drill where someone has to fall through 3ft of ice into a frozen lake and use their skis to drag themselves out – with all their kit on their back – the

Mountain Leaders in charge of the demonstration will be lying on the ice with sunglasses and budgie smugglers on, an inflatable pink flamingo by their side as they top up their tan.

I've never forgotten that particular training session. Humour makes learning more memorable, which allows the student to better retain the information and be more effective at the task they are asked to complete. It commands the student's attention and they remember it, perhaps because of the shock of the unusual, perhaps simply because it has more positive associations that the brain wants to hang on to. Any reputable memory guru will tell you that one way to enhance your memory is to make the things you want to remember bold, vivid, colourful and funny. Nobody remembers the mundane. I know many leaders will seek to put up a shield, unwilling to crack a funny because they mistakenly believe it shows weakness, but as a leader of men I know that showing your own vulnerability is a strength and we need more leaders in every aspect of life who are willing to go to that place – to engender a cheerfulness that will allow people to feel at ease, to feel free to make mistakes and then ultimately to give their best. Feeling at ease with a certain level of vulnerability can be directly linked to humour and the ability to laugh at yourself. We 'crack a funny', have a wry smile and share our mistakes, making sure others learn from them as well as yourself.

Those instances of unforgettable shared humour can also create moments that last for a long time and create a special bond between people that can be invaluable for a family, social group or workforce. That sense of a mutual understanding and cheerfulness is a sure-fire way to see relationships mature and blossom, even when handling moments of crisis. A positive and cheery attitude also helps us to step back, pause and handle an intense situation with the calmness required to make sure the best outcome is reached. Sometimes when we get too serious and emotionally intense it can cloud our perception and damage relationships because ego has got in the way of clear, objective and clinical judgement. So if there is room for a little levity, try and bring it to the situation.

In your circle of friends, colleagues and family, I challenge you to be that person with that cheerfulness, that thoughtful word of joy to change the mood. Small acts of cheerfulness soon add up and can change the dynamic of a family, or how a business operates, or even someone's life that seems to be heading on a downward spiral. You can be the Marine in your friendship or work group, responding with cheerfulness during adversity and making a real difference to people's lives.

CHAPTER 10: CHEERFULNESS LESSON SUMMARY

Remember ...

◆ The ability to not take yourself too seriously and laugh at yourself is key.
◆ A sense of humour is a great tool to help you get through tough times.
◆ It often takes just one person to radiate cheerfulness to lift all the others around them.

Step 1 – WHAT is cheerfulness?

Cheerfulness is a persona characterised by being happy and positive.

Cheerfulness in adversity is when humour is used to maintain morale despite the overwhelming challenges that we may face.

Step 2 – WHY is cheerfulness important?

Cheerful promotes happiness and being happy enhances productivity. A cheerful life is therefore also a productive and fulfilled life. To be cheerful is to embrace life and to enjoy it. Cheerfulness also develops a positive mindset, which leads to clarity of thought and an openness to build meaningful relationships with others. Cheerful people tend to live life to its fullest.

Step 3 – HOW to be more cheerful in your life.

- Being cheerful is a conscious choice – choose it above pessimism.
- Focus on the positives in your life.
- Develop your ability to laugh at yourself – especially when things aren't going as you hoped.
- Find your passion in life – it will make you more likely to be cheerful.
- Lift the morale of others through a single act of cheerfulness.

CHAPTER 11

Integrity

Definition: The quality of being honest and having strong moral principles.

Why me? That was my abiding thought as I stood to attention in the fabulous London 2012 Olympic Stadium along with seven other military personnel selected as Olympic flag-bearers at the closing ceremony of the Games, surrounded by celebrities and some of the best sportsmen and women on the planet.

An estimated 23 million in the UK were watching along-side one billion across the globe and here was a boy from south London playing a key part in the official handing over of the flag into the safekeeping of the 2016 Rio Games organisers – the final curtain of one of the most successful Olympics ever.

I have always seen myself as an ordinary man who at times has had the opportunity to do some extraordinary things in life, and this was certainly one of those times. That moment, as we stepped out into the Olympic Stadium of 80,000 people, was one of the most fulfilling of my life. It felt like the culmination of all that I achieved to that point, and I felt incredibly honoured to be given that responsibility.

As a lifelong sports fanatic, I couldn't have been more excited but, more importantly, it was an incredible privilege to carry the flag representing the five continents. It was a moment that will remain a family legacy for my kids and grandchildren to be proud of forever.

Wondering why I had been selected ahead of tens of thousands of other servicemen and women – many of whom have served their country with distinction – for this prestigious, once-in-a-lifetime opportunity, I looked at the others around me and realised that everyone here had one value in common: integrity. Lives lived with integrity at their core will often reap the rewards further down the line – with the kind of bucket-list moments that you only really dream about.

Taking the hard path

At the Olympic ceremony that night, it dawned on me that life is a series of connected moments, linked by the choices we make. When we talk about integrity, we have to talk about making decisions. Life is a series of decisions, and how you make them will determine who you are and what kind of life you lead. In my experience, when you try your best to do the right thing, when you believe in others and when you seek out role models who show the highest levels of integrity, that's when the good things start to happen. But the path to get there is often not the easiest one.

In my experience, those with high integrity are the opposite of those who are always looking for the easy path in life. They are usually industrious and driven, delivering their best in whatever task they are handed. They don't shift blame or pass the workload to others and then take the credit. Instead, they do what they have been asked and are ready to do what's right, rather than what's easiest. Ask yourself now, honestly, if you believe that is the level of integrity you are living out? Are you taking the right path, or the easy path?

In the Marines we engage in a great deal of map-reading so we are able to navigate through the hardest conditions across difficult terrain. Sometimes the right thing is to navigate through a swamp or over a mountain. There's always a reason behind this decision; often in the Marines it is to avoid enemy detection and to save lives. It may not be the easiest way, but it is the right way. A combination of both instinct and experience will play a part in your decision-making, but only by assessing each situation on its merits can you work out the optimal route to take. The metrics will change depending on the situation, but some of the questions you might need to be asking yourself are: what are the long-term consequences? How does this affect others, besides myself? Is there anything about this that makes me feel uncomfortable, or doesn't sit well with my core values?

Once you have assessed what the right decision is, the next and hardest step is to follow through with it. It can be easy to convince yourself that the easy route is in fact the right route, but you must try to maintain the standards you set for yourself and avoid this kind of self-deception. When you begin making this argument to yourself, pause and challenge it. Ask yourself those searching questions again. Be alert to the possibility that you are trying to deceive yourself. You will know – there will always be a little niggle, a small voice saying that this isn't the right path.

It takes an incredible amount of hard work to maintain your integrity. Sometimes you might slip from these standards – human beings aren't perfect and we have all compromised ourselves at one stage or another – but the key is to recognise the slip. Acknowledge that you let yourself down, and redouble your efforts to not let it happen again. This shows integrity in itself, as you possess the honesty to recognise that you have moved away from your standards in the first place. If you find yourself continually slipping, then maybe you need to readdress your decision-making process – are you asking yourself the right questions? Are you challenging yourself? Do you need to sit down and redefine the core values that inform your decisions?

When it comes to making these decisions, how we frame the process is important. Choosing the right path in your life rather than the easy road takes dedication and commitment, but that word 'choosing' is crucial: it's about choice, not sacrifice. People who achieve their goals often speak of the tough decisions they had to make to be successful, missing out on things like parties with their mates or eating fast food. This is especially true with elite athletes, who give up many luxuries in order to focus solely on their careers. But the ones who are really successful do not resent this. I first saw this mindset in play when working with Team GB athletes. They talked openly about the privilege of representing their nation and told me it was not a sacrifice but a conscious lifestyle choice they were making. That perspective of choice rather than sacrifice dramatically reduced the feeling of missing out on what is seen as a normal lifestyle for the rest of society.

Drawing your lines

Integrity is having the moral courage to sometimes say no, or to take an unpopular or difficult decision because you believe it is right. It's about being honest with yourself and sticking to your personal values. It's a personal conviction that will not allow you to act against your core beliefs, regardless of what others around you may do or say, no matter how bitter the pill is to swallow.

We will all face challenges to our integrity at some point or another. The temptation to bend or break the rules and so damage your integrity is never far away, whether it be the successful businessman dodging taxes, the teacher giving that extra mark to the pupil he or she naturally favours, or the politician being economical with the truth. But how do we resist such temptations? The truth is that it is your choice. When you feel tempted by something that you know isn't right and contradicts your values, pause and make the time to assess the potential consequences of your action. Each time you resist the temptation, you will strengthen your willpower and you see your resolve increase. The additional carryover benefit of this type of integrity is that it is also a great way to grow your self-discipline and mental fortitude.

Integrity is in the small actions, not just the big ones. The most difficult challenges can in fact be the ones that seem unimportant, the ones where you can convince yourself that it won't really make a difference. No one will know. It doesn't really matter. Sometimes it's easier to let the little things go, such as allowing your kids get away with something you know to be wrong, but that often leads to confused boundaries and more complex problems further down the line. Because when you allow integrity to slide in the small matters, the big ones won't be far behind.

In the Royal Marines, we are taught about the concept of an ethical bridge, spanning the divide between what is wrong and what is right. It is a metaphor that so clearly applies to every walk of life. It's easy to creep across that ethical bridge without being aware that you are suddenly on the wrong side of it. Each step is small, but it is the ultimate destination that counts. That's why any sign of slippage of ethics or moral code is quickly jumped on by the Marines.

When someone breaks their own ethical code, that can lead to deception in other areas of life. Succumbing to pressure and choosing the wrong path can become a habit, just like anything else, and before you know it, the personal integrity of that man or woman has been eroded. It is consistency that keeps you on the right side of the ethical bridge.

The Royal Marines have developed their value of integrity based on their ethics. Ethics are the values and principles that guide the behaviour of people in relation to their duties; companies often articulate their own 'code of ethics', which is a written statement regarding the values and principles that guide its members in line with organisational beliefs. Similarly, you can have a code of ethics in a family or even a social group.

As a Marine, an employee, a family member, or simply as a member of society, it is worth taking the time to build you own ethical code by thinking about where you stand and where your own boundaries are. Link them to the importance of your core values, clarify the way you will conduct yourself and make a vow to yourself that you're going to live them out every single day. You can then consciously draw your 'battle' lines and make a commitment to yourself that you won't ever cross them.

Check your flashes

Staying on the right side of the ethical bridge is something we can help each other with, by holding each other accountable.

During the course of a career in the Marines, you will say or hear the words 'check your flashes'. It refers to the Commando badges that we earn and wear on each shoulder, and it is a phrase used when someone falls short of our levels of integrity. It's a gentle, non-confrontational reminder to look at 'who you are' and to maintain your high standards of integrity so that you don't accidentally – or purposefully – compromise them. It's essentially a respectful way of calling someone out and, importantly, it can be used both up and down the chain the command – so you could tell your boss to 'check his flashes' and it wouldn't be seen as insubordination.

Once it's been said, that somebody will address whatever the particular issue is with the Marine in question, because it has to be nipped in the bud right away.

Often, this useful phrase need only be said once and the person in question will realise that they have strayed out of the acceptable boundaries of our moral code and will instantly rectify the issue and get back on course. The power of communicating in such a direct yet respectful way leads to the rapid resolution of issues before they fester and grow into a more serious problem. This demonstrates the importance of setting clear boundaries, ensuring everyone knows where they stand.

Even if you all know the boundaries, it can still be difficult to hold each other accountable. Having worked with businesses across multiple industries, I've seen situations where employees are afraid to engage with their boss in this way, even if they have witnessed them breaking their own boundaries of integrity. It's so important to be empowered to 'do the right thing', but sometimes it may seem daunting to call your boss out as it may feel like overstepping the mark, or you may worry that you may be unfairly disadvantaged in your career as a result. This is why a trigger phrase like 'check your flashes' is so useful. It doesn't imply any judgement or criticism; it is a very simple reminder. I've seen teams from sports and business adopt their own version of the Marines 'check your flashes' quote to good effect, as their own method of non-hostile communication both up and down the chain of leadership and command. It's effective, it's respectful and it works.

It is extremely helpful to be accountable to other people, to have someone remind you to check your flashes. But integrity is also something that you are doing for yourself. Integrity can sometimes appear performative – doing the right thing so that others will see you doing it. This is not integrity. True integrity can often be invisible, quietly holding to your own moral code. The celebrated British writer C. S. Lewis summed it up best when he said, 'Integrity is doing the right thing, even when no one is watching.' This said, integrity is highly valued by other people, who will be quick to recognise it in you. Integrity is directly linked to your reputation and cannot be compromised, otherwise it affects and dilutes every other value that you may stand for.

Being honest and reliable

An important aspect of integrity is being honest – first with yourself, and then with those around you, as they need to know that they can rely on you, no matter what. This is especially important in situations where you put your life on the line for each other, such as Marines in combat. You have to trust the men at your side and rely on them to be there for you, especially when things go wrong, when the enemy is close or when you find yourself in the dark looking for a way forward. Under such pressures, when life throws you a curveball, this is how you find out who has your back – and who hasn't.

Sometimes, retaining your integrity can mean not making the promises you wish you could make. I can recall incidences of senior officers promising Marines who had been blown up by IEDs and were severely injured on the battlefield that they will be looked after 'for the rest of their lives'. This is something that is impossible to follow through on 100 per cent, despite being well intentioned. Broken promises only lead to a breakdown in trust and integrity.

Reliability in your day-to-day behaviour is equally important. Young recruits are under no illusion that actions outside the norms of behaviour are, from the standpoint of integrity, not acceptable. Unpredictability can be a matter of life and death in the Marines. That is why consistency of behaviour is expected. Some people can be referred to as 'Billy Two Heads', because you don't know what side of the bed they will wake up on from one morning to the next, and of course that impacts on how they treat people. That inconsistency means they are hard to work with and leaves others walking on eggshells in case their behaviour or comments are interpreted the wrong way. I bet we all know people like this. In the Marines, that inconsistency can compromise missions and cost lives; in the workplace or home life it can lead to untold stress.

To maintain integrity, therefore, you must do all you can to be reliable, otherwise those around you will start to doubt how genuine you really are. A reputation built over many years can be lost in a moment.

Integrity in leadership

Integrity in every part of society is what we are badly in need of, but it is particularly important at leadership level, as this has a trickle-down effect on the rest of society.

In the Marines, each recruit is linked by reputation to the one who trained them, and if they slip from the standard of integrity that has been set, then the question will always be asked: 'Who trained you?' There is therefore a deep sense of accountability, personally and collectively, and that's what we need an abundance of in society, more so now than ever before.

I don't think we have to look any further than our reigning monarch for a role model of such an important value. Ultimately the head of all the Armed Forces, Her Majesty Queen Elizabeth II has an unquestionable integrity, and any time I have been in her presence I have felt inspired. Our monarch leads by example, and immediately commands respect because her selfless service is plain for us all to see. The Queen places everybody ahead of herself, she doesn't seek the limelight and she has never acted in an improper way. Quite simply, she exudes an unwavering integrity that should be embodied by every true leader.

Sadly, the same cannot always be said for many in positions of high office across the globe, many of whom seem to be caught up in the blame game and who display a lack of personal responsibility that is the opposite of integrity. How refreshing would it be to hear a political leader say, 'Look – hands up, I made a major mistake. I apologise and I'm doing everything in my power to rectify it now'? That level of integrity would raise levels of behaviour across society, because within that there is a sense of genuine respect for one's fellow men and women.

Athletes have the opportunity to demonstrate integrity every time they compete. Parents have the opportunity to express integrity every time they make promises to their kids. Leaders have the opportunity to show integrity every time they communicate with those they are privileged to lead.

Integrity in conflict

Integrity reflects the ethics of an individual and an organisation, and that's why the Marines have lectures on ethics – to make sure no dents in our standards are allowed through. Those standards remain the same regardless of how challenging a situation we find ourselves in. In fact, as is the case with so many of these values, integrity is even more important in a conflict situation.

The Marines integrity shines like a beacon when it comes to engagement with the enemy. When deployed in Northern Ireland against the lethal threat of the IRA, it was imperative that we followed the rules of engagement – that our integrity as a fighting force was upheld despite the extreme provocation orchestrated by the Provos in Republican areas.

This came to the fore in Belfast, 1989, when out on patrol. As you can imagine, during the Troubles it was imperative that we conducted ourselves in a proper manner in line with the law of armed conflict. We knew the enemy would not live by the Geneva Convention, but that didn't mean that we had to follow suit. So when, as part of a routine foot patrol, I happened to meet the West Belfast Commander of the IRA, I didn't – as I could have – mess him around or try to embarrass him with a strip search for example. Instead, I showed him respect as a combatant and we had a chat – both of us knew what we believed in and where we ultimately stood. Our ideologies were completely opposed, and I could not respect his ideals, but according to my own principles, and those of the Marines, I had to offer him the respect due to another human being. I'm sure he felt the same way towards me. Looking back, this encounter taught me that you can still respect the integrity of people even if you fundamentally disagree with their foundational principles.

This is not easy – especially if the other person doesn't afford you the same courtesy. But remember that integrity is about holding yourself to *your* standards, not matching the standards someone else is displaying. The phrase 'don't sink to their level' is often used – and it's true. Remember, you set your own levels for a reason.

Integrity, intelligence and respect

It speaks volumes about the integrity – the strong moral principles – of the leaders of the Marines, particularly during the time I passed through training in the late 1980s, that I never encountered any racism. It's one of the main reasons that I went on to serve for over three decades. There was an unrelenting consistency from my instructors that no matter who you are, you are going to be judged on what you do and how you conduct yourself, as opposed to your creed, colour, religion or orientation. It's not light and fluffy, people say what they mean and sometimes that is some pretty tough straight talking, but there is a core of respect and integrity, meaning that certain boundaries of acceptability are never crossed.

Discrimination of any sort is unethical, cowardly and unintelligent, and does not sit alongside any of the Marines' core values. Royal Marines are renowned for being the thinking man's soldier, and that level of intelligence translates directly to how we act – both on and off the battlefield.

The instructors know that they have a position of power and it would have been easy for them to pick on an individual for all manner of reasons. But they never did abuse that trust and I know that this is because the basic fundamentals of being fair and honest are so embedded in the organisation. Everyone gets an equal chance to show what they can do and respect is earned from the way in which we conduct ourselves, no other reason.

The Marines recruit from a whole range of different backgrounds and upbringings from around the world. During the selection phase, we assess only for potential because we realise that some have had less exposure to life experiences and less access to role models, whereas others have been more fortunate. Young recruits join with all different ideas and values; some join with very few or none. When I joined up I had no real idea what integrity meant and no understanding of how important personal values were. But the instructors taught, coached and mentored me and my fellow trainees, taking the time to explain the ethos of the Corps and its history, its traditions and its values, and why this was important. They didn't want us to blindly follow the values of the Marines – they wanted us to understand *why* we were doing so.

The key to maintaining the integrity of fairness in training is undoubtedly based on the quality of the instructors and training staff who are hand-picked from a cast of many to be responsible for the prestigious role of training new recruits. And so it continues, the infinite line of green beret mentors passing the beacon from one to another.

I am so fortunate to be surrounded by family and special friends from all sorts of backgrounds, and everybody is given 100 per cent respect. That's the way it is in the Marines and that respect can only be chipped away if a person does not offer the same integrity in return. I'm very proud of the fact that the Marines have always been a forward-thinking, adaptive organisation and this is reflected in their modern-day thinking and training practices. The recruits now have lessons on unconscious bias and I knew the importance of that, especially in my later years as Officer Commanding the training. It was brought in as a competence that had to be learned in the same way that you learn weapons competence.

The integrity of the whole organisation is maintained by constantly referring back to the standards expected of each individual who dons the green beret, but also by constantly revising and updating these standards. It is a living, evolving moral code that has been fashioned throughout the Marines' 350-year history: it drives us, it defines us, it unites us. Our identity stands for something special that we all buy into, whether that is the youngest recruit or the most senior veteran. The definition of Royal Marines integrity will forever be linked to its strong identity and unwavering moral principles.

United in integrity

Each Royal Marine is accountable for his brother and sister to the left and to the right of him – a ring of integrity made of steel. It is that same kind of integrity that we have sought to bring into our marriage and family life.

As a team my wife Suzanne and I are responsible for instilling values and beliefs into our four children, such as not telling white lies just because that's the easy option. Being a parent is one of the toughest jobs in the world – I think every mother and father would agree on that. That's why integrity in the home is so critical to the development of our young loved ones.

Unclear or shifting boundaries are extremely confusing – for anyone, but particularly for children – and can easily lead to problems. Being aware of those pitfalls, Suzanne and I make sure we act as a team when it comes to discipline and uphold the same standards. So, when it comes to chastising our children, it is done after we have come together and talked the situation through. That way we come from a united position of strength and, more often than not, make the right judgement call, rather than an instantaneous decision based solely on emotion. We re-enforce those critical boundaries together as a team. As well as Suzanne's strong family values, many of our principles also come straight from my experiences in the Marines: owning up to mistakes and learning from them, speaking truth even when it hurts and sticking to your ethical standards even when others around you are happy to live by a lower standard and compromise their own values and beliefs.

Looking back over my life, and the people I've met who have shown great integrity, I have come to the conclusion that it is what I would class as a bedrock value, one which is uncompromising and set in stone. It needs to be part of your character, something that has clearly delineated boundaries, but which still allows for development and growth. In fact, I believe that integrity underpins many of the other key values mentioned so far and forms part of that inner belief system we all have which determines who we are and what matters to us.

CHAPTER 11: INTEGRITY LESSON SUMMARY

Remember ...

- People with integrity choose to do the right thing, even when it's hard.
- You can't fake integrity, but once you have it then people will inherently recognise it and trust you.
- Someone with true integrity knows that everyone deserves respect.

Step 1 – WHAT is integrity?

Integrity is the quality of being honest and having strong moral and ethical principles.

Step 2 – WHY is integrity important?

Integrity allows us to broadcast the best version of ourselves no matter what situation we find ourselves in. People with integrity are comfortable in their own skin, they trust their own judgment and they consistently do the right thing – even when no one is watching them. It is integral is growing your personal belief system.

Step 3 – HOW to develop integrity in your life.

- Do the right thing, especially when no one is watching you.
- Don't hide. Become open for the world to see and speak up for your values – it will enlighten you.
- Find the conviction to maintain your personal standards, even in the face of opposition, and always be reliable in this.
- Realise that you aren't perfect, you will make mistakes. So, recover quickly, check your flashes and get back on track. You will be stronger for it.
- Get the little things right and the big things will follow. This is where the magic starts to happen.

CHAPTER 12

Excellence

Definition: The quality of being excellent.

It may sound strange, but some of the best Marines would have made great gangsters – and who knows, I could have been one of them. The Marines put me and many, many others on a path in life: the path of excellence. We say that when you get home and take off your green beret, it's still on inside you. It is always part of who you are. In the same way, excellence is a way of life – something you strive to reach every single day.

A life of excellence is something that everybody can have – no matter what your starting point. Marines take recruits from every part of society and give them a chance to succeed in life and my life bears testimony to that. During the eighties I could often be found on the terraces at Millwall, along with my group of pals, and I have to admit there were come scary moments. Guys with face masks on, eager for trouble, and some carrying meat cleavers so they were ready for mayhem. For young men from housing estates, the lure of the gang is intoxicating and the lifestyle attractive. Growing up in a tough neighbourhood, with no excitement or purpose in their lives and very little money, a gang offers them excitement and a sense of belonging. It's addictive, looking forward to the next game – the next scrap with opposing fans. This is the reality for many, and it was mine for a short time when I was young, immature and inexperienced.

I recall one of my old Marine mates. Originally from south London, as a teenager his life was going down a similar track to mine. But, also like me, the Marines took him on a different journey, and it would be one of excellence. I had heard of him during my Millwall days but only really got to know him as a Marine. In the Marines he changed and learned to be a fine leader, just as I had to. He became not only one of the most esteemed commanders but deservedly got all the way to the high office of senior leadership. He ruled with an iron fist but was wholly respected by all. Everything he did was of the very highest standard and he demanded that same standard from everyone else. He is just one of dozens of very tough men that I have had the privilege to serve alongside, and every one of them decided to choose the right path in life: the one that leads to excellence.

Substandard behaviour, leading to mediocrity rather than excellence, is sadly not hard to find in our society, and it leads to a mountain of unfulfilled promise. Too many young people are being left to accept low standards of behaviour as the norm and their environment becomes a self-fulfilling prophecy of a gang culture riddled with crime and substance abuse. It doesn't have to be that way. As hard as it can be, parents and those in positions of authority in society have to do their best to set standards that see beyond such an environment and recognise the potential. And the same is true for all of us. While you might not be leading a life of gang crime and violence, it is worth asking yourself: are you leading a life of excellence? Or have you settled for mediocre?

Setting high standards

The 350-year history of the Marines is interwoven with excellence. And excellence within the organisation starts with excellence from the individuals. Every day, I set out my stall to demand excellence from myself in whatever I am doing that day. It's a personal decision, and no one is holding me to it but myself, but I'm never happy with anything that falls short of the highest standard. And when you make a pact with yourself to aim high, then striving for excellence becomes a habit – a good one! You may not always get there, but that doesn't stop you from doing everything in your power to be the best you can. Aim for the sky of excellence and at times you may fall short and land on the trees, but aim for those low branches and you could easily end up flat on your back.

So the first lesson in achieving excellence is: don't be afraid to set ambitious goals. Your goals should reflect the excellence you want to achieve. They might not currently be within your reach, but that is, after all, the purpose of a goal – it is an aspiration. If we only ever aimed for targets that were already within our reach, then we would never grow, never improve, never achieve excellence. As former US Marine Sergeant Major Michael Mack states: 'You have to have goals in life. If you fall short, then at least you have achieved something. Nothing good will ever come easy. Your focus must be on excellence.'

A life of excellence is one with a purpose, and without goals there can be no purpose. Without goals there can be no plans. Without plans and things to look forward to, life can become meaningless. In the pursuit of excellence, therefore, you will need to set specific, measurable goals, and I would suggest they come from the heart. Find something that matters to you and you will be more likely to put everything that you have into it. It could be that qualification at work that you've wanted to achieve, or that extra bodyweight you've wanted to lose, or even that college course you always wanted to start, but never did.

Remember, and this is crucial, your goals are personal to you. They shouldn't be based on what society, or those around you, consider a success. As Mack says, 'I may not be an astronaut but I can lead a healthy life, be a good neighbour, honour my family and leave a great legacy as a father, husband, son and Marine!' Excellence is in the high standards you set within those goals, not in how impressive they sound.

Set excellence as the ultimate standard for achieving all your goals, and by doing so you will remove any limitations from what you think you can achieve in life. Maybe that does mean becoming an astronaut. Maybe it means running that 10K. Maybe it means being the best partner/parent/friend you possibly can be. Once you've set some big goals in your life that matter to you, the next step is to create smaller process goals that will help you achieve the bigger ones. It can be daunting to look too far ahead, so create mini-steps and keep your goals achievable and realistic within the context of what you want to accomplish. The fulfilment of your dreams has to start somewhere, right?

By embarking on a new journey with a purpose you will find out a lot about who you are, and then things will really start to change. You will be more aware of what talents and skills you have, and by setting challenging goals for you to aspire to, you find that you can use your abilities to best effect. Excellence in your life is a case of striving to live the life that is beyond the standard you previously set for yourself. It's about growth.

This only comes through hard work. But throughout the grind, always remember: you were designed to be excellent; excellence lies within you. The key is to learn how to unlock it and fulfil your potential. It will take both commitment and immediate action, but by fulfilling that potential, you will realise that you can do it, that it was worth all the effort, and that you can achieve anything you set your mind to.

Attitude not talent

You can change your life, especially when you come to realise that there are no limits. Once you do that, change starts with choosing what you do and how you do it – every single day. There's no point committing to change then procrastinating while waiting for the first step to happen by itself. *Now* is the time for that change to take place – not tomorrow, not next week. It starts with something small, then it grows, and all of a sudden, your new actions become the norm.

The most satisfying aspect of a life lived in the pursuit of the gold standard is seeing your own personal growth and development. Put simply, you become better, and once you make that pledge toward excellence, it will naturally spread into other areas of your life.

This is about attitude, not talent. As Sir Clive Woodward says, 'Talent alone is never enough,' because possessing a positive 'get up and go' attitude will drive your willingness for change and allow you to move forwards even when the path might not be clear. By demanding excellence of ourselves, however, we change our view of the world, one step at a time, and trust me when I say that anyone can do it.

I saw this 'get up and go' attitude in the England women's football under-20 squad when they came to the Marines training headquarters in Lympstone in 2018, just a couple of months ahead of their World Cup finals campaign. They were led very skilfully by the wonderful Mo Marley, a former England captain, and it was clear from the start they were hungry for information and for success.

These girls impressed me so much because they didn't come with egos; they just wanted to excel in every way. As we put them through the training course they were open to learning at every turn and were willing to put everything they had into the process. This was reflected in both their physical and social attitudes. Not only did they push themselves exceptionally hard in physical training, they also realised and accepted that to push their standards ever higher they needed to get to know each other better, to understand one another and that would then lead to a higher standard of performance driven by the mantra of 'One Team'.

The period of reflection at the end of the training, when we split them up into groups, enabled the squad to pause and reflect upon the qualities of each member of the squad, to see what was working well within the group and what could be improved upon. They reassessed their standards, pushed them higher, and committed to achieving and maintaining these standards as a team. The whole team had a humble attitude and a willingness to learn, and as a result they managed to raise their level of excellence on the biggest stage of all, deservedly going on to win their first-ever bronze medal at the under-20 World Cup.

Of course, striving for excellence doesn't stop there, it becomes a lifelong pursuit. As it grows, you can begin to 'dare to dream' of those things you once thought impossible. It was incredibly rewarding to watch many of the women from the under-20 squad go on to blossom at the European Championships in 2022, becoming the first England senior team to win a major trophy since 1966. Winning is a by-product of when you get the little things right, and with that comes success and recognition. Watching this team forge ahead, breaking new boundaries and making history is something that I am proud to have played a small part in. It is amazing what can be achieved when you develop a winning mentality, based on the values we have explored in this book, and where aiming for excellence becomes the norm.

Failure

I've worked directly with hundreds of Olympic champions, World Cup winners and captains of industry in my time, yet one thing that I have noticed that they all have in common is failure. For winners, however, such setbacks are never permanent. They may have all failed at some point in their lives, yet that has not stopped any of them from getting back up and taking the next step forward.

This requires a combination of resilience and mental fortitude, which is how forward progress is made. Successful people know that excellence and failure often go together. It is a theme we have visited many times over the course of the book – simply because it's so important to understand and threads through the life and values of all successful people. My greatest successes have come just the other side of fear and defeat, and if you think it's too hard to pick yourself up or that it's not possible to bounce back, then you should think again.

No one is denying that failure hurts. However, it's the detailed reflection and subsequent learning that will allow you to reassess your goals and try again. Any failure should always be followed by a pause – taking a tactical knee, that idea we've already touched upon. When you take a pause, you can remind yourself of WHY you're doing this, WHY you want this, reinvigorating that desire to achieve your goal. This is followed by a period of honest, detailed reflection. Why do you think you failed? What could you have done differently? What could you have done better? You then need to build the lessons you've learnt into a new and improved route forwards. This will allow you to use your experiences, both good and bad, to develop a new plan aimed at achieving your goal with the pursuit of excellence at its core.

I think it's fair to say that everybody wants to be a winner in whatever they do, and at every stage the Marines make sure that this is ingrained in every challenge you face in training. I can still vividly remember my first day of training more than thirty years ago, when we were lined out to compete in an uphill sprint race up the so-called 'beasting knoll' against the other sixty recruits. The non-commissioning officers told us that, in life, it 'pays to be a winner' and that we had to get familiar with being put in a position where we were expected to excel. So the sprint began, every recruit racing against the others to the top. Only the first two frontrunners got to stay at the top; everyone else had to slog it back down to the bottom. Then we all sprinted again and the next two frontrunners stayed with the winners from the previous race. We raced again and again until, eventually, everyone was at the top.

Of course, most times you lost the race and had to trudge back down the hill to do it again. This taught me three things. Firstly, you should try your best, put in every ounce of effort from the get-go and make sure you are the winner – to take the uncertainty (and drama) out of the situation and be first. Secondly, if you fail, then you'll always get another chance. Thirdly, and most importantly, there is often someone better than you, so pick yourself up, stay humble and keep your feet on the ground.

Just as everybody wants to be a winner, nobody wants to lose. That feeling of failure is surely one of the most agonising experiences in life – it stays with you, it marks you, and you remember it! However, avoiding failure at all costs can lead you to become risk averse and unprepared to take any chances. This is a natural reaction and one which we are not overly comfortable with; we can tend to dodge opportunities where we feel there's a chance we might fail and 'get found out'. This is closely linked to feelings of 'imposter syndrome' where you may feel you don't belong or maybe you don't feel ready to explore new opportunities yet.

Some people suffer from imposter syndrome when they believe that their success isn't deserved and that their skills aren't up to the task. It can cause anxiety, stress and a sense of not feeling up to the task in hand. The first step to overcoming imposter syndrome is to take ownership of your own successes. Of course, it is right and proper to recognise the many others who may have played a part, and to keep a humble attitude, but imposter syndrome strikes when this goes too far and you don't recognise that your own talents and hard work played any part at all. So acknowledge everyone who helped you, and then take a look at the part you played. What did you do well? What did you work hard at? What can you be proud of?

It is important to knock imposter syndrome on the head because it affects how we go into our next challenge and whether or not we set out with the confidence and determination to achieve our next goals. Perception plays a large part in this, and perception is, crucially, subjective; sometimes a pre-conceived idea of what awaits us might not be right. So many examples spring to mind where I've worked with individuals whose perceptions were clouded through fear of failure, especially when they encounter the unknown.

When entering an unknown situation it's important to keep an open mind and to adopt a can-do attitude. Don't write yourself off as unable to cope before you even know what challenges lie ahead. As Head of Performance, I've hosted literally thousands of visitors to our Commando Training Centre and you could smell the trepidation and fear of most of the visitors who enter through the gate, whether they were recruits, schools, business people or sports teams. The perception was that they were going to get shouted at and made to do thousands of press-ups and pull-ups while being snarled at by burly Marines, and that they weren't up to the challenge. Nothing could be further from the truth.

Sometimes, of course, your preconceptions may prove correct, but in all likelihood they will not; you will have exaggerated the situation out of fear and apprehension. In the case of our visitors at the Training Centre, their perception was completely wrong. They soon found that we hardly shout at all; instead, we encourage, nurture, guide and mentor, and do everything that we can to inspire and support someone's aspirations and dreams, whatever they may be. Almost all of them leave having achieved things that they never thought they were capable of. Things aren't always what they seem and an unfounded fear of the unknown can waste valuable energy.

Nobody ever wants to fail and feel stupid, but avoiding what you really want to achieve is not the way to go about it either. I've noticed in life that many are told, or choose, not to stand out and to just blend into the background, which is the safe option. But these 'self-limiting beliefs' are counter-intuitive and limit progress. By being too afraid to fail, you are naturally feeding the part of you that is averse to taking any chances and therefore you are removing the opportunities to grow and excel. This type of outlook often results in mediocrity at best.

Being a 'grey man' was never an option for me; it simply does not appeal. Of course, it's never easy, but to aim for excellence you must be prepared to stand out, to put your head above the parapet and risk the chance of failure. You must be prepared to raise the bar, to take calculated risks and to dare to dream. That is where the magic starts. So, the challenge for YOU is to aspire to new and unexplored levels where you think and act in a manner that demands the very best of you.

Attention to detail

I have noticed that real excellence always lies in the detail – the depth of hard work, the background effort, the training, the revision, the effort to get yourself out of bed. It's often the work that no one sees that makes the difference – all those little extra details amounting to something very significant. It may take a little while, but once you start to see the results, you will realise what a positive effect the choices you made – big and small – have had. That will then give you new confidence and inspire you to become self-disciplined enough to make excellence a consistent habit in your life.

Put simply, you have to be prepared do the things that others won't do to have the successes that others won't have. In the Marines, for example, we train to lie in cold, wet bushes for hours and days, ready to spring an ambush at an opportune moment. This requires us to practise being uncomfortable so that you don't twitch or make the slightest noise that could alert an enemy patrol. It also requires patience – a lot of it! In reality, one mistake could get the whole team killed, so we train in a way that our enemies may not. We go the extra mile and we 'train hard to fight easy', so that gives us an operational edge against an enemy when we do it for real. We've exposed ourselves to harder training, so we're better prepared, we've got better people and better leaders. The effort goes in NOW and we reap the rewards further down the line. That's exactly where we need to be if we want to have the edge over an opponent, an enemy or a competitor.

I've seen this type of mindset in the sporting world as well, in the form of top athletes who know that to remain an elite performer they have to put in more focused, detailed training than their competitors otherwise they will be overtaken. In today's world, many teams have psychologists, physios, specialist coaches, analysts, nutritionists, Michelin-star chefs and incredible facilities. But they also know that the differences between teams are so narrow that it will often come down to the smallest gains – the attention to detail, the mindset and attitude. To gain that kind of competitive edge, you must be prepared to do things a little differently to your opponents, thereby gaining new experiences from which you can draw at a later date. That's why the highest-performing teams seek inspiration from organisations such as the Marines.

Maintaining those high standards

In the Marines the pursuit of excellence is something that we commit to and then act upon. It's not something we try out and then give up on a few weeks down the line. It's not a New Year's resolution. It's about devoting yourself to a new way of life – one where you make a pact with yourself to do the very best you can in everything that you do, whether that is cooking the evening meal, cleaning your house or playing for your local sports team. Every day.

One place where I feel there is no hiding place for this is in the family home. Straight away I hold my hands up – like every parent – to making mistakes, but that doesn't mean that high standards do not prevail. I annoyingly (for them) repeat to my children on a regular basis that 'PRACTICE MAKES PERMANENT'. Often you hear the phrase 'practice makes perfect', but this isn't quite true. The reality is that practising forms a permanent habit, so the consistency of how you live out your standards is what will ultimately be your badge of honour.

I recognise that people have different approaches to bringing up children and organising their family life, and I am not here to judge anyone else. For us, the Marine way of excellence is one that Suzanne and I have sought to bring into our home – high standards have to be set and those parameters and boundaries are critical. Consistency of example from us as parents is crucial because if you slip from your own standards then credibility and authority is fractured – we see this in every walk of life, whether it is politicians breaking COVID-19 regulations or business leaders having one rule for one employee and a different rule for another. Without consistency in life, children suffer, they struggle to develop without consistent, high standards. Children don't just organically develop the right morals and standards, they need guidance – they will set their standards according to what they see practised by the adults around them. It is imperative that they know the parameters in the same way that as Marines we are taught what is acceptable and when you have crossed the line to the point of being sub-standard.

It's the same for adults too, we need to set our own boundaries and standards in our lives – whether they are moral, physical, emotional or social – and be consistent with them. By setting boundaries we establish our tolerance and limits. It's all part of living a life of excellence. It requires dedication, passion and commitment, and it's far from easy.

Excellence in leadership

The Physical Training branch of the Royal Marines defined the majority of my career and we often talked about aiming to reach the 'gold standard'. PTIs are in the top 1 per cent of the Marines and it's tough to get in. The corporals and sergeants responsible for delivering PT will consider the attributes of certain Marines and refer to them as being 'of the gold standard' because they deliver to the highest level over and over again – they are delivering excellence on a consistent basis. The man who took me on my Physical Training course and showed me what a new level of excellence really means was former Colour Sergeant Ade Cole. He is someone I hold in very high esteem. He demanded the highest standards from us, and he could do so because he performed to an impeccable level in everything he did. He always led from the front as a shining beacon of what is possible. If you're going to demand the best from someone then you have to demonstrate that you are all about giving 100 per cent. Leadership falls down when excellence is asked for but isn't in evidence – whether that is in behaviour, how you communicate, how you dress, or any aspect of your life, no matter how minor it may seem. Ade never gave anyone an opportunity to point a finger of criticism because he took seriously his position as teacher and role model to those he was instructing.

I joined the PT branch in the 1990s, by which point I was a senior Corporal. The move up to this specialised role as a Physical Training Instructor meant that I would be taking on additional responsibilities. The more responsibility you take on board, the greater the importance of having and maintaining that standard of excellence. People are looking to you to lead them in how to act and behave. Planning and preparation were going to be key. Being able to answer any question that was going to come my way was now crucial, so I needed to work hard, knuckle down and gain that knowledge so that I could now perform as a mentor and coach just like Ade. The only way to go to this next level was through hard work and commitment. It may sound flippant but that is the truth.

One aspect of Ade's leadership style that I particularly liked was that he would not only emphasise the benefits of hard graft, but also clearly highlight and set out ways for you to improve. Ade taught me that it's a combination of knowledge, skill and a good work ethic that enable you to take your 100

per cent up a notch. This is where a constant growth mentality is very important because you need to be open to learn,
you need that humility, in order to keep stretching your 100
per cent mark. You should never feel that you cannot grow or
improve further. In my view there is no such thing as 101 per
cent, but you can and should be aiming to grow your 100 per
cent to new levels every single day. A closed mind will never
be able to do that. It doesn't matter how old you are, there
is always something more to learn and discover and with the
right mindset you will continue to progress far beyond what
you initially thought you could achieve. There is no limit to
what is possible.

Ade gave all of himself to the men he was teaching. He
would show where in the past he went wrong and then
explain how he learned from his experience and did it better
the next time. Sharing your mistakes and being prepared to
show your vulnerabilities is demonstration of the highest level
of leadership. Excellence isn't about being perfect in every
task every time; it is about seeing how you can keep raising
the bar – and not settling for a lower standard which you
know is not giving your all.

One such man who embodies the qualities and values of
Royal Marines and has a reputation for always striving for
excellence is former Colour Sergeant Stevie Hargreaves. I
have had the privilege to work alongside Stevie on operations and exercises around the globe and he was also a highly
respected Physical Training Instructor who typified the 'Gold
Standard'.

But it wasn't always like that for him. What turned things
round for Stevie was the way in which the leaders within the

Marines engaged with him, demanding excellence from him, *expecting* it of him, and working alongside him to ensure he achieved it. Stevie explains:

> I was thrown out of school then college, I didn't like who I was as a teenager, not a person of value. I was a right little s**tbag, I used my intelligence poorly, I was half the size of everyone else, I was a year ahead at school, but squandered the opportunity and I went down a bad path, turning into someone I really didn't like.
>
> Having been thrown out of college, I joined the Marines. I had respect for Royal Marines. People used to say that I couldn't handle discipline, but the people teaching me (up to that point) in my life hadn't engaged with me, they hadn't talked to me, they hadn't earned my respect.
>
> So, I was happy to go to an organisation (like the Marines) that would give me the discipline that I needed. I had no interest in being mediocre. It's why I joined the Marines, to provide me with a platform that enabled me to become something and ultimately someone better. It was the first time that I'd been good at anything, I got a superior pass, and was offered a spot in a recruit troop as soon as I could join. The Corps demonstrated a faith in me and immediately gained my loyalty, by making me feel like I could be of use. For the first time in my life, I was going to add value to an amazing organisation.

Stevie's story gives us all some encouragement that we can excel with the right role models to follow and with the right type of encouragement. The Marines had earned Stevie's respect through their outstanding leadership, so he engaged and he changed, and once he started to believe that he had found something he could excel at, he excelled.

The Royal Marines gave me this code of excellence, which is the value that I seek to bring into every single aspect of my life. It's something that I would recommend for every family, business or whatever context you find yourself in because it draws upon all the other values we have discussed in this book and elevates them.

So, what standards have you set for your life? Can you aim higher to get out of that rut and progress in life? Now is your starting point for living the values discussed in this book, setting new standards to strive for, acting on them and then witnessing how the by-product of excellence transforms your life.

We should never stop challenging ourselves or put a ceiling on the standards that can be reached. Priorities may change as we live out our journey, but standards don't. That's the mindset that transforms a life – it's the way of excellence that we all need.

CHAPTER 12: EXCELLENCE LESSON SUMMARY

Remember ...

♦ Excellence and failure often go hand-in-hand.
♦ Achieving excellence is about attitude, not talent.
♦ Always strive for the 'Gold Standard'.

Step 1 – WHAT does excellence look like in your life?

Striving for excellence is a crucial tenet of high performance. It means setting ambitious targets, always pushing yourself that step further and never settling for mediocre or even 'good'. The goal is to incorporate excellence into your life so that it becomes a self-sustaining habit.

Step 2 – WHY is excellence is worth aiming for?

By taking your values and standards to new levels, you'll notice that your personal and professional growth will expand exponentially, and excellence will become its by-product. This will improve both your reputation and your life.

Step 3 – 'How' do you incorporate excellence into your life?

♦ Incorporate your 'why': what drives and motivates you? Use this thought to understand why you need to be excellent in all that you do.

♦ Remind yourself what skills you possess that will help you to succeed.

♦ Form a clear plan with process steps on how you are going to attain your goal.

♦ Reflect honestly on your performance and apply any learning (on what worked and what failed) into your next task.

♦ Apply hard work and see it through to the end: above all, Never Give In.

CONCLUSION

Living it

Now it's time for you to live these values – to live life like never before.

The Royal Marines has shown literally hundreds of thousands of new recruits that the right mindset can transform their lives – and that mindset has twelve deep-rooted values at its core. It stands tall, free of the shadow of self-limitation and leaves behind the shackles of years of unfulfilled dreams and desires. Now is the time to discard that narrative of self-doubt and replace it with a mindset that sees you breaking through into a virtuous new world of possibilities.

If you are looking to change your life for the better, then you have to develop and improve what you do and how you do it. You will always be a product of what actions you take on a daily basis. You can truly change your life when you live in accordance with the values we've discussed here. I can say that because I have lived it and will continue to do so.

We all start this journey at different points. That might be a tough place or it could be a solid base. Maybe you feel you have no foundation whatsoever and life seems to be stuck in reverse. You cannot change your starting point, but you can change the way in which you move forward, refusing to believe the mistruths that you may have already been told in life, that have put a ceiling on your goals, dreams and potential. It's time to shake off these limitations and the mediocre way of living that they create and to start demanding more of yourself through the framework of these twelve Marine values. Whatever your goal, and from wherever you start, I would call on you to embrace the values we have discussed in this book that will allow you to move forward in the right direction.

Whatever stage of life you're at, this is a journey you can take. Now in my fifties, I have new goals and 'bucket lists', new challenges I want to take on. For the rest of my life I will not let go of that growth mindset where anything is still possible, and neither should you. So, find a chink of light, build that inner confidence and know that you *can* do this. Believe me – anybody with the Marine attitude can move forward and achieve in life if an ordinary person like me can do it!

When I understood there was no ceiling on my life, it made my impossible dreams achievable. But it isn't just about the outcome, it's also about what you put in: whatever I achieved, I would only be satisfied as long as I could look at myself in the mirror and say that I gave every last ounce of effort.

The training in the Marines pushes you beyond your limits and shows you the power of the mind, allowing you to achieve what you previously thought was beyond your grasp. When tight situations come along, it teaches you to find the determination and self-discipline to just keep putting one foot in front of the other and to seek to live a better life, in ways both big and small. All of your ambitions and dreams are just the other side of your comfort zone. This is what it means to live out these values that, when embraced, will keep you moving forward towards your goal.

After thirty-two years of service, I may have left the Royal Marines, but the identity and values have never left me. The connection and bond with these values and the men and women who bore testimony to them on a daily basis is as strong as it ever was. It is who I am.

The sense of belonging and identity within the Royal Marines starts with the posters they have up on the walls listing the values we have covered in this book. They are everywhere, displayed proudly as a constant reminder of what you stand for. I suppose you could say it was a form of indoctrination, but in a positive way. When it came to actually 'living it' as a Marine, we were shaped by the combination of the Commando mindset, Commando values and Commando spirit. These values on posters would come off the wall and be imprinted on your heart and mind, and after months of training together and bonding, the mindset, values and spirit become part of your personal central belief system. It becomes your ethos.

The shared nature of these values is critical. A real sense of belonging and identity is something that every human seeks – we have a natural desire to be part of something bigger. You see it with supporters of national sporting teams or when we witness the outpouring of love or grief for an iconic sporting legend such as Muhammad Ali or a world leader like Nelson Mandela. These are people who transcend their own worlds and somehow people feel an attachment to, through shared values such as hope, peace and kindness. These men didn't just talk a good game, they lived their values.

One of my good friends, the highly acclaimed Owen Eastwood, is someone who has helped me a great deal as a mentor since I left the Marines and moved into civilian life. This sense of identity and belonging is very close to Owen's heart. Having started life as a lawyer, he has gone on to carve out a highly successful career as a performance coach, working with many top high-performance sports teams. In 2021 he released his first book *Belonging*, in which he explores how a sense of identity, formed through shared beliefs, is fundamental to success in people and teams, as well as contributing to a life filled with purpose and contentment.

Owen says:

As human beings we are hard-wired to need to have a tribe to belong to, that as a group of people share an identity and to be a member of that group that share the same values.

When I was five years old my father died. He was part Maori, the indigenous people of New Zealand, and part English. When he died it felt to me that was the end of the connection to my Maori heritage. It felt that something very special, very precious had been broken because he had passed away and I was very hurt and restless about that. I felt I was close to being part of something special but I wasn't. So, when I was twelve, I wrote to the Maori tribe that my father belonged to and they wrote back and for me it was an amazing, transformative moment when they said I belonged with them as well, I was part of their tribe.

The Maoris have a spiritual idea known as whakapapa – that each of us are part of an unbreakable chain that goes right back to our first ancestors and also stretches ahead into the future, to the end of time. We are all interlinked and the Maoris understanding of this is that the sun shines on everybody over time – today it is you but the sun has slowly passed down over each generation of the tribe.

I invited Owen on a visit to the Royal Marines to watch the ceremony for the passing out presentation of the green beret to every recruit who had successfully completed the training. In our celebration of the latest members of our band of brothers he recognised the same ethos and understanding behind the Maori idea of whakapapa.

Deeply understanding shared values is critical, and that's why every time you walked down a corridor in the Marine barracks or you went to work out in the gym, the posters were there to remind you about the qualities that were expected of you as a Marine. The culture and ethos were shining beams of light in your life everywhere you went. When I bought into those shared values and beliefs, and really embraced them in everyday living, I realised that I had found my tribe. There was a sense of respect for myself and others that was wrapped up in this new sense of belonging. It was instructive to me and has been a source of inspiration going forwards in my life.

Ask a Marine what are the core values of the organisation and every one of them will be able to tell you without hesitation because they are 'living it'. Having words on a poster on a wall is one thing, but taking them from a wall and placing them into hearts and minds so they are lived out is quite another. When I go back to where I grew up in south London, I sometimes see people throwing rubbish on the floor or letting their dog poo and just leaving it on the ground and I just can't stand by and say nothing, I can't let it go. The easiest route would be to turn a blind eye, but if everybody did that then the community ethos breaks down and those shared values are lost.

In line with the values discussed in this book, getting the small things right will have such an impact when it comes to the bigger issues. Living out these values means you apply them in every area of life, right down to what may seem such a menial task. That old well-worn phrase, 'If a job's worth doing, it's worth doing right' really does apply when you're seeking to maintain high standards and instil positive norms of behaviour in your life.

It can be easy to become entangled in a lifestyle that erodes the values that, deep down, we do know to be best practice. Once again, I urge you to build into your life at regular intervals the Marine practice of taking a tactical knee to pause and reflect. This can help you to press the re-set button and once again consider who you are and the person you want to be, emanating the values that will contribute to a better society, a better work or family environment. It is important to regularly pause and ask yourself, what are the values of your business? What are the values of your family? What are the values of your community? What are the values of your school?

When working with the England football team it was very

interesting to see how frequently they paused to reflect on who they are, where they were going and what values they were living out. This was constantly changing, hence the need for regular reflection. There was an awareness that society is always developing and so the old ways to connect and inspire the current crop of players had to develop alongside it. An organisation has to be open to change without losing touch with its long-standing identity and values. The same is true for individuals – for you. One person has observed that the Marines are a collection of different personalities but with one mindset or as I would put it, the Marines bring together individuals and moulds them into having the one ethos.

I hope the same is true of my family and how we live out our lives, both together and separately. It's not about being the perfect family – we all know that doesn't exist – but it is about shared standards and beliefs that we know are to the benefit of all and will stand up to the test when things go wrong, and how we will overcome. This applies both to the small acts that make up everyday life, and to life's bigger challenges. It's the Marine way, but it's also our family way, and this means so much to Suzanne and me. Suzanne is the glue that keeps the family together – and I would say she's an honorary Royal Marine; she's earned that accolade over many years. The Royal Marines shop sells a t-shirt which cheerfully sums it up: 'If you think it's hard being a Royal Marine – then try being a Royal Marine's wife'.

My wife Suzanne knows all about the Marines ethos: 'These values are a reality in Scott's life. The sense of integrity in everything he does shines through. Scott sets very high standards and will always tell you the truth whether you like it or not. Failure or making mistakes is not the end in Scott's eyes because that's how we learn.'

The Marines are very good at inspiring people and when I reflect on why, it is because they walk it like they talk it: they are living out these values. The people who have inspired me most in my life have all had a genuine approach to how they dealt with people, and over time that has built up a trust and life-long connection based on shared values and experiences. Our officers train directly alongside our men. Indeed, if you tell them that you can't do something then they will immediately show you how you can. When you realise this to be true it is a game-changing moment in your life – suddenly anything becomes possible. What an inspiration that is, what a hope for society, if that's the message from our leaders: that nobody gets left behind, that anything is possible – for anyone. Remember that: it may be that you're stuck in a rut at the moment, but that doesn't have to be the case forever. There is always an opportunity to change for the better, sometimes you just need someone to show you how – I hope this book can be that guide for you.

So many people, probably billions, are being lied to every day. One of the greatest lies we are told, and perhaps that we tell others, is: 'You can't do it.' You may have heard variations of this, such as: 'You're not smart enough,' 'You're not strong enough,' 'You'll never amount to anything,' 'You'll never make it.' This book is here to tell you that this is not true: you *are* enough, in every way! You can break free of these false restraints by pledging yourself to a life without limits, where commitment, dedication and hard work become the norm and where you create and sustain a new lifestyle with these twelve values as your bedrock. With such endeavour comes reward and recognition.

I have lived these values for more than thirty years and they have brought so much richness into my life: adventure, achievement and recognition, but also friendship, respect and pride. It was the Marines that made this happen for me, but you don't need to be in the Green Berets to live out these values and reap the rewards. They are within all of us; they just need to be liberated, and that will only occur when you make the conscious decision to change and improve your life. By reading this book, you have already taken the first step – congratulations!

So go out there and live out the Marines values. You will soon find that there is no limit to what YOU can achieve. Because as we have seen, the Marines is all about building a state of mind where you believe anything is possible and you never, ever give in.

It's the Marine way.

ACKNOWLEDGEMENTS

Having completed my first book, I feel humbled and blessed that so many very special people remain a huge part of my life going forwards. Whilst writing this book, I very quickly realised that my story is not just about me, but is also about the incredible people with whom I have had the privilege to brush shoulders as part of my own journey.

My special family and close friends are the cornerstone of our combined long-term success and I feel so blessed to have you in my life. My career would not have been possible without the love and support of my family, especially Suzanne, the love of my life. That love has filtered down into our children who have all gone on to be successful in their own right. Seany, Marico, Casey and Charlie, I love you all and I look forward to meeting future generations of our family for whom this book was written as part of the legacy to keep the Commando spirit and values alive in our family!

Never has a day passed in the writing of this book that I don't think of my dearest Nana and Grandad, Edie and Harry Mills. They remain a shining beacon of light for me especially when things don't go as you would hope.

I thank my mum Vivien and siblings for nurturing my competitive spirit as we were growing up. My brother Tim is an inspirational artistic talent who looks at everything from a different viewpoint to me – together we are so strong and his impact on me has brought out the very best. Our sister Lola is a shining light of what can be achieved when you truly live your values. She is one of the most talented and loyal people I have ever encountered, and her positive spirit is an inspiration to us all. My youngest brother Alex is supremely talented and high intellect and strong family values have propelled him along a path where he believes anything is possible. To my siblings, I love you all, and our combined sixteen kids have kept 'Grandma' very busy in her retirement years.

To Suzanne's mum and dad, Dave and Sally, and all their descendants, I thank you for accepting me as one of your own and for the love you have always shown to me.

To the officers and men of the Royal Marines, past and present, you have inspired me every day to live out the values in this book. There's too many to mention but YOU know who YOU are . . .

To Lee 'Frank' Spencer, Baz Barrett, JJ Chalmers, Dan O'Mahoney, Mark Scoular, Jock Hutchison, Lara Herbert, Michael Mack, Owen Eastwood, Peter 'Louis' Lewis, Tony 'Screwy' Driver, Stevie Hargreaves and George Stephenson, I thank you so much for your insights into the Commando values – you have inspired me and I feel so honoured that you have contributed to the book. To Adam Smith, Rob Richardson, Tony Phillimore, Terry Barton RIP, Laura and Gary Jones, Marc Birch RIP all of you would have featured heavily if this book were an autobiography.

To my many friends in the field of elite sports, the players, coaches, psychologists, medical staff and technical staff, I thank you for inspiring me to write this book, shaping out the multiple crossovers and linkages between the Marines values and success in sports, business and in life. To Pippa Grange and Owen Eastwood, thank you for your example, friendship and leadership in guiding me through the transition from the military into your world; I shall not forget your support.

Lastly, a huge thank you to my literary agent The Blair Partnership, publisher Simon & Schuster, and the many key influencers who have helped to shape this book.

I thank you all so much . . .

'Never Give In'